anted Here's to you Never sleeping through From

ed Before you ran Before I knew it You were trying

t on your own now somehow SLOW DOWN Won't you

ough the door But it's all too fast Let's make it

nna fly I am your biggest fan I hope you know I

's to you Every missing tooth Every bedtime story

unday Had to crawl Before you walked Before you

g love can Hold hands through it When it's scary,

e more I know you want to walk through the door

inted to the sky and now you wanna fly I am your

u can somehow SLOW DOWN   ll your

ll understand You'll hold   em

n But do you think you can Somehow SLOW DOWN

Here's to you You were pink or blue And everythin

midnight till the morning Had to crawl before you

to free your fingers from my hand 'Cause you could

stay here a minute more I know you want to walk

last a little while I pointed to the sky and now y

am But do you think you can somehow SLOW DOWN

Here's to Barbie cars, light saber wars Sleeping in

ran Before I knew it You were teaching me The only

you've got me SLOW DOWN Won't you stay here a m

But it's all too fast Let's make it last a little while

biggest fan I hope you know I am But do you thin

eyes at me I know I'm embarrassing But someday

if they can I am your biggest fan I hope you know

To: ....

From: ....

Date: ....

Slow Down

Embracing the Everyday Moments of Motherhood

NICHOLE NORDEMAN

THOMAS NELSON®
Since 1798

Published in Nashville, Tennessee, by Thomas Nelson. Thomas Nelson is a registered trademark of HarperCollins Christian Publishing, Inc.

Interior design: Milkglass Creative, LLC

Thomas Nelson titles may be purchased in bulk for educational, business, fund-raising, or sales promotional use. For information, please e-mail SpecialMarkets@ThomasNelson.com.

Scripture quotations marked ESV are from the Holy Bible, English Standard Version·. Copyright © 2001 by Crossway, a publishing ministry of Good News Publishers. Used by permission. All rights reserved.

Scripture quotations marked THE MESSAGE are from *The Message*. Copyright © by Eugene H. Peterson 1993, 1994, 1995, 1996, 2000, 2001, 2002. Used by permission of NavPress. All rights reserved. Represented by Tyndale House Publishers, Inc.

Scripture quotations marked NIV are from the Holy Bible, New International Version`, NIV`. Copyright © 1973, 1978, 1984, 2011 by Biblica, Inc.` Used by permission of Zondervan. All rights reserved worldwide. www.Zondervan.com. The "NIV" and "New International Version" are trademarks registered in the United States Patent and Trademark Office by Biblica, Inc.`

The excerpt from Shauna Niequist's book in the essay "Cheating on Santa" is from *Present Over Perfect* (Nashville: Zondervan, 2016), 130.

ISBN 978-0-7180-9901-5

Printed in China

17 18 19 20 21   DSC   10 9 8 7 6 5 4 3 2 1

FOR CHARLIE AND PEPPER

I AM YOUR BIGGEST FAN.

I'VE GOT YOU.

Mom

contents

foreword

SHAUNA NIEQUIST

Sometimes at a baby shower, the hosts will ask each mom to write down one piece of advice for the expectant mama—and we all write things about sleep or feeding or how desperately hard it is to deal with those onesies with snaps in the mind-altering middle of sleepless, blurry nights. But then I also write one more thing as well: whatever you do, don't do it alone.

Mothering is life altering, soul altering, identity altering. It is physical and emotional and spiritual. It's alternately breathtaking and boring, a treasure chest of all the best things in the world and a set of endless tasks, a delight and a dizzying weight to carry.

And the only way I know how to embrace motherhood—the best and the worst of it—is to spill it all out to the other mothers in my life, over the phone or across the table or in books and stories.

Nichole's beautiful song "Slow Down" connected with so many of us so deeply and so immediately because she says what we all want to say, and she makes us feel less alone and less crazy for feeling those things. She captured that feeling, that nothing-like-it-in-all-the-world, this-is-just-exactly-what-it-feels-like-to-be-a-mom thing, and we needed every note of it.

Because that's what helps us through: the sense that we're not alone in the enormity of motherhood, the sense that we're not the first or the last to feel like our hearts might actually break with love. For many of us—for me, anyway—to know that we're not alone in the wilds and wonders of mothering is a game changer. It's a life changer.

A band of women have walked this mothering road with me—through joy and loss and sleeplessness and fear and hospitals and stitches and silliness—and I cannot thank them enough. Nichole is one of those women, a fellow mama bear, a songwriter, and a storyteller who captured the beautiful ache of motherhood so absolutely perfectly—a true friend who carries it all with me.

Through these pages, you'll meet friend after friend, fellow traveler after fellow traveler. Our children are so different, our homes and traditions and paths are so different, but mothering is mothering: challenging and desperately beautiful and so much better together.

the black keys are better

A couple of years ago, my son, Charlie, was getting ready to graduate from elementary school. His teachers and many of the fifth-grade parents at our small school were dreaming and scheming about ways to make the brief graduation ceremony meaningful. After all, we were about to bid farewell to elementary school musicals, science fairs, and pumpkin patch field trips and launch our fresh, new middle schoolers into the world of large lockers and math we could no longer help with.

I did something I never do. *Never.* I asked Charlie's teacher if I could sing at the ceremony.

I'm not kidding when I say that my own family can barely get me to start "Happy Birthday" in a decent key while my aunt is blowing out her candles. I've spent the last two decades writing and recording music as a Christian artist. I've logged a lot of miles on tour buses and planes and stood on many stages, large and small. Like anyone's job, mine can be a great gift and a grind at times. When I'm not performing on the road, I never volunteer to sing at anything, for any reason—very rarely at my own church.

But I asked, gingerly, over e-mail. "Would you mind if I sang at the fifth-grade graduation?"

The teacher agreed to include me, and then I forgot all about it for several months. The week before the graduation ceremony, I remembered (and regretted) my offer. I was certain Charlie would be super embarrassed. I had no idea what to sing. "Wind Beneath My Wings"? What would I even say to the kids? What if I started bawling? What was I even thinking? The next time you feel pretty good about what a cool mom you are, try standing in front of a roomful of middle schoolers, and tell me how fantastic you feel about any part of your outfit or personality.

"Mommy!" he'd announced. "Come see! I colored all the keys black! *The black keys are better!*"

In the end, I decided I'd sing a song called "Legacy" that I'd written and recorded a decade earlier, hoping it would encompass the spirit of "go forth and make your mark on the world, young people." Charlie would just have to work out his embarrassment in therapy years later.

The night before graduation, I sat down at my keyboard to brush up on "Legacy." I played through the song once or twice, and at one point during my late-night rehearsal, I glanced down at my hands and noticed black Sharpie marks on some of the keys. I'd stared at those marks for so many years that my eyes had grown accustomed to the "creative coloring" Charlie had done when he was three years old.

"Mommy!" he'd announced. "Come see! I colored all the keys black! The black keys are better!" I came around the corner to see him covered in permanent marker and to behold his handiwork on the keyboard I've owned for more than twenty years: the beloved instrument upon which I've written every one of my songs. The songs that have won awards and accolades. And the college songs that were so bad, Jesus Himself would have to white-knuckle it through the first chorus. If my house went up in flames, I would try to save this keyboard before the cat.

Thanks to Google, I'd found a way to remove most of the marker, except for some little scribbles that still remained, my fingers now frozen over them.

Charlie's little voice rang in my ears. "Mommy! Come see!" And in an instant, I did see. I saw every moment: from diapers to crawling to walking to tooth fairies to Santa to karate to training wheels to bicycles to black Sharpie to drum lessons to Legos to trick-or-treating to Pokémon to science fairs to basketball practice to the end of fifth grade. Just like that.

In an instant, I did see. I saw every moment: from diapers to crawling to walking to training wheels to trick-or-treating to the end of fifth grade.

One large box of tissues and many photo albums later, I abandoned my decision to sing the safe, familiar song and wrote a new one. I sobbed, as I am sobbing now, to think of it.

The moments we never get back. The moments I was always trying so hard to rush through.

Please be done breast-feeding. Please give up the bottle. Please hurry and eat solid food. Please sleep through the night. Please outgrow your pacifier. Please take your first step. Please say your first word. Please hurry, hurry, hurry, and do the next thing that the baby books and blogs say you are supposed to do.

Oh, God. Please let me build a time machine in my garage so I can go back.

Please. Slow. Down.

And out tumbled the lyrics that became my "Slow Down" song for Charlie and his little sister, Pepper, and inspired the book you now hold in your hands. I had no real intention of recording the song at all. People smarter than I am talked me into that decision, as well as the beautiful idea to compile a simple video of new and old friends and the moments they most wish they could slow down with their littles.

Nearly twenty-five million views later, I better understand why "Slow Down" went viral. It's the universal plea of parents. We all want to slow time and make the most of every tick of the second hand. How could I have known, late one night at my piano with my full and achy heart, that I was giving so many other people the language for such tender places in their own families' lives?

I walked onstage the next morning, looking out at Charlie and his classmates—boys sitting respectfully in awkward starched shirts and ties; girls with French braids and lip gloss. I don't remember exactly what I said, something about asking them to be patient today with us moms and dads if we squeeze them too hard and for too long.

I caught Charlie's eye. He was nervous for me. He gave me an anxious

The moments we *never* get back. The moments I was always trying so hard to rush through.

smile . . . like the one he's seen from my seat every time he took any stage. As I cleared my throat and forced my hands to move nervously over the grand piano's pristine ivory, I wished every one of those keys were black.

Deep breath.

Don't miss this moment.

Slow down.

Here's to you.

slow down

NICHOLE NORDEMAN, CHRIS STEVENS

Here's to you
You were pink or blue
And everything I wanted
Here's to you
Never sleeping through
From midnight till the morning
Had to crawl before you walked
Before you ran
Before I knew it
You were trying to free your fingers from my hand
'Cause you could do it on your own now somehow

Slow down
Won't you stay here a minute more
I know you want to walk through the door
But it's all too fast
Let's make it last a little while
I pointed to the sky and now you wanna fly
I am your biggest fan
I hope you know I am
But do you think you can somehow
Slow down

Here's to you
Every missing tooth
Every bedtime story
Here's to Barbie cars, light saber wars
Sleeping in on Sunday
Had to crawl
Before you walked

Before you ran
Before I knew it
You were teaching me
The only thing love can
Hold hands through it
When it's scary, you've got me

....

Slow down
Won't you stay here a minute more
I know you want to walk through the door
But it's all too fast
Let's make it last a little while
I pointed to the sky and now you wanna fly
I am your biggest fan
I hope you know I am
But do you think you can somehow
Slow down

....

Please don't roll your eyes at me
I know I'm embarrassing
But someday you'll understand
You'll hold a little hand
Ask them if they can

....

I am your biggest fan
I hope you know I am
But do you think you can
Somehow
Slow down
Slow down

you make me want to be brave

I was a total wreck of a brand-new mom. I did all the new-mom stuff they warned me about. It's almost too cliché to type it all out: Read too much. Bought every trendy gadget. Obsessed over books and blogs and consulted every last mom, aunt, grandmother, sister-in-law, and friend in my circle for advice on sleeping, feeding, swaddling, scheduling—all of it. Each woman's hard-earned, golden wisdom directly contradicted the hard-earned, golden wisdom of the friend who had just enlightened me thirty minutes prior. All the books disagreed with each other.

In the spirit of self-compassion, I will remind myself now that I had an extremely unhappy baby. Charlie had a condition called gastroesophageal reflux, which is a fancy way of saying that he projectile-vomited every ounce of liquid or food he consumed for the first eighteen months of his life. He also never slept for more than three to four hours at a time because he was constantly hungry. So my life was a twenty-four-hour cycle of baby barf, inconsolable crying, and zero sleep. Most days I looked at tiny Charlie and just wept. Eventually I was prescribed an antidepressant, which meant I wept slightly less.

For some reason, the only time—the *only* time—Charlie would stop screaming was when his dad or I would hold him in a steamy shower. Between the two of us, we basically showered about fifteen times a day. It was hell. But it was a clean hell.

My friends would call and want to get together with all the mom friends and their babies for a lunch date. I didn't understand the concept. *Like, you guys are going to put on mascara and stuff and then order food and eat it, and your babies will be sleeping with pacifiers in their carriers? What does that even mean? What is this* lunch *you speak of?*

I had never felt so frail. So inept. So alone and small. My friend Shannon drove by our apartment every day and left the same voicemail. "Hi. Your blinds are closed again. Have you even left the house? Are you okay?"

One day her voicemail changed. "Hi. If those blinds are still closed when I drive by today, I'm beating down that door and airlifting you out. I'm not playing."

During this season when Charlie was a few months old, my friends and I threw our friend Alison a baby shower. Charlie's aunt Bean flew in from out of state to help with him, which consisted of taking him out in the stroller for hours so he could scream outside instead of inside during the baby shower. Alison was pregnant with her first child, and we wanted to celebrate her, although truthfully I had decided at this point that baby showers were kind of a sweet joke that everyone but the new mom was in on.

You guys are going to *put on mascara* and stuff and then order food *and eat it*, and your babies will be *sleeping* with pacifiers in their carriers?

What is this lunch you speak of?

While we watched Alison open booties and blankets and nibbled delicately on mini muffins and smiled at her, all I could think about was when I could grab her by the arm, shove her into a dark closet, and whisper dire warnings of what she was about to encounter. I felt guilty about oohing and aahing over Alison's new crib sheets when a real friend would set her straight. Thankfully, I restrained myself from this encouraging speech.

Afterward, while washing dishes at the sink with Alison's mom, I mumbled something nice (and true) about what a great mom Alison would be. And her mom got very quiet and serious and said, "You are right, Nichole. But it's going to be very, very hard. And you know this now. Bringing a baby into the world is one of the bravest things a woman could ever choose to do." She said it slowly and soberly, not in a baby-shower voice.

It is an extraordinarily brave choice
to say *yes* to new life.

It was the first time I had felt seen by someone since I embarked on this agonizing, soul-exposing journey called motherhood. It was the first time someone wasn't patronizing me with some hopeful "this too shall pass" speech or another mind-numbing suggestion about how to swaddle tighter.

Alison's mom was right. It *is* a very brave decision to grow a human and then bring that life into the world and make a way for both of you. It makes no difference if you squat in a field or a cave in a developing country, give birth on eight-hundred-thread-count sheets at the Ritz, or open your arms as another mama courageously hands you her child to call your own. It is an extraordinarily brave choice to say yes to new life.

Motherhood isn't some rite of passage. It's not just what women do. The cry of a mother is the cry of a warrior.

When Alison's mom said those words to me, I felt hot tears of exhaustion sting the corners of my eyes. I took my hands out of the soapy water, dried them, grabbed a pen and a baby-shower napkin, and wrote the words that would become my own song to him later. "Dear Charlie, you make me want to be brave."

Not sane. Not nicer. Right now, certainly not happy and barely okay. *Brave.*

big love

JEN HATMAKER, *NEW YORK TIMES* BESTSELLING
AUTHOR OF *FOR THE LOVE*

I quit my job to stay home when I had my second baby just after her big brother turned two. Those first few months as a SAHM (stay-at-home mom) to two were, let's say, mildly traumatizing. I used to call my husband, Brandon, at 1:30 p.m. and ask, "Are you almost done with work?" and he would be all, "It's 1:30" and I would be like, "*You didn't answer the freaking question. Are you on your way home, or should I call 911 to come help me manage these two babies?!*" Because no one told us not to, Brandon and I added a third child two years later and were ruled by the tiny army we had created.

Three babies in four years—it was a whole thing.

I wish I would have known how new babies make all feelings *more* (and this from a girl who was already fairly high on melodrama): more thrill, more love, more anguish, more adoration, more fear, more gratitude, more doubt, more crazy. You may have been an emotionally sturdy professional just a minute ago, but a newborn takes your heart and mind, squishes them into pulp with her fat little baby hands, and turns you into a woman facedown in despair over a Subaru commercial. *Who is this sloppy woman in the mirror? Put on some clean pants, and get your crap together!*

I remember a watershed moment the second year of staying home with the littles. Brandon came home from his glamorous job (*glamourous* here meaning "out of the house") and found me sitting at the kitchen table, staring blankly. The kids? Not sure. I wanted to say they were . . . upstairs? The backyard? They were somewhere on the property. My gosh, I wasn't in the FBI.

Brandon, speaking slowly, as if to a lunatic: "Um, hi. You, uh, you okay there?"

"Fine. Everything is fine. Except that I've turned dumb. It's fine."

"What?"

"Dumb. Now you have a dumb wife. I used to be smart. I watched CNN. Did you know that I went to college and graduated with honors?"

"I did know that because I met and married you there. Remember?"

"Well, sorry for your loss, because now I'm dumb. I sing the theme song to *Blue's Clues* when the kids aren't even around. That's what I do now. I eat their leftover bread crusts off the floor. I can't remember the name of our vice president. I told our neighbor I was twenty-nine."

"You're twenty-seven."

"Thank you for *confirming the diagnosis, Mr. Fancy Job*."

Some days were very much like that. Raising the littles was sometimes the most frustrating, boring, numbing, exhausting, lonely job I'd ever had. But also, the opposite.

The Feels were all big, including the good ones. As I type this, I can literally recall how the littles' chubby little cheeks felt against my lips; I kissed them hundreds of times a day. I remember exactly how my heart surged seeing a smiling, white-haired baby standing at the crib rails, squealing at the sight of me. I precisely remember all their first steps; I was there, cheering and laughing and holding out my arms to the first son at twelve months, the girl tot at thirteen months, and of course the "spirited" baby at nine months.

When I could push through the Big Exhaustion and Big Guilt, I tapped into something healthier: Big Pride. Every night with three precocious littles fed, bathed, read to, rocked, snuggled, and tucked into bed, I felt like some sort of warrior princess. Who can handle this many babies and toddlers all day? *Apparently I can.* (And if

I managed to also have sex that night? I felt like a viable candidate for the Nobel Peace Prize for my contributions to humanity.)

You can handle motherhood too, Young Mama. The new-mom brain can be a real enemy, saying you are not enough and falling apart and a hot mess. But look at your children. Their shoes are on the correct feet, at least one has combed hair, those round bellies are clearly well fed, and peek into their little eyes: lots of light in there, Mom. Those are the eyes of loved, cherished, cared-for babies. You're doing it. You are raising whole humans, healthy and happy and safe.

Can I tell you what happens next?

First, you will get your groove back. Your dumbness will abate. Your brain will return, and it will come back wiser and less judgmental. (Unlike that older lady in the store as my toddler pitched an epic fit for Count Chocula cereal: "My children never behaved that way." *How nice for you, and may I offer my condolences to your daughter-in-law.*) Not us, gals. We get it now. We love all the young moms behind us. We buy their wine on airplanes and encourage them in Target as their tot takes off his pants and streaks down the aisle. We tell them how our two-year-old once bit her Sunday school teacher and drew blood and assure them easier days are ahead.

And they are!

Well, easier in most ways. Guess what? Kids grow up and pee-pee on the potty! They make their own sandwiches! They wash their own hair! They go to school for seven hours a day! *I'm serious.* The nonstop physical parenting slows down. The daily marathon relents.

But I have some bad news too. These little ones? You will fall even more madly in love as every year passes. That part doesn't get any better. Subaru commercials are still out to kill us. The Big Feelings stay big, especially the tender ones. Your brain becomes useful again, but the kids grow up and you cannot stop it. That beautiful three-year-old you're tucking into bed? Blink, and you'll be sending him to driver's ed.

Let me tell you about Big Feelings: My oldest son, the one who took his first step into my arms at twelve months old, is wrapping up his junior year of high school. One more year and he launches. I can hardly speak of it. It went so fast. People told me it would, and I didn't believe them, but here we are in the home stretch; the finish line is near. The Family Years are waning, and it literally takes my breath away. (Brandon says the kids are just growing up, not dying, but I'll cry about it *if I want to*.)

I'll tell you something most moms don't: teenagers are mostly awesome. Sure, you want to strangle them, but they are funny and smart and interesting. This teen stage is totally my jam. It's not all great—this exact minute my husband and son are inspecting a fence he plowed over, hot-rodding through puddles with his best friend last night—but no stage of parenting is all great. Young Mama, set that future fear aside. You will adore that baby when he is one and eight and thirteen and donning his cap and gown.

So, what I wish I would have known before bringing that first son home? The baby years are short, kind of like five minutes . . . underwater. It doesn't seem like it, but he will go on to kindergarten, then read the Harry Potter series, then join the "ninja club" in middle school, then play high school soccer, rent his first tux for prom, and run over a fence with his truck. And near the end, you will hit your knees and thank God that you got to parent this kid, that he is yours, that he walked into your arms at one and will walk out of them at eighteen, but my gosh . . . what a gift. I wouldn't trade one day of Big Feelings because the good ones far outweigh the hard ones, and the one that endures above all else is Big Love.

bravery in vulnerability

Sometimes being brave in my brand-new mommy months meant being a lot more vulnerable with people I trust. It's sounds counterintuitive, right? Bravery usually means a stiff upper lip. For Christian women especially, the pressure to smile through life's valleys as a public tribute to our faith (as though God feels more honored when we deny our emotions) can be very real. But being vulnerable liberates us. It allows us to drop the act with the people who weren't buying it anyway.

This is true of motherhood across all ages and stages. When we level with the trusted people God has placed in our paths for specific seasons, we give ourselves the gift of their tenderness.

being a brave mom means:

▸ **Acknowledging that shepherding a child's life is an astonishingly brave choice.** You are choosing a life of surrender to something much greater than yourself. You are saying yes to the raw and tender places; yes to insecurity and uncertainty; yes to grave vulnerability. And while you are saying yes to one million other joyful, beautiful moments, you have put yourself squarely in the path of love's wrecking ball.

▸ **Owning the non-brave moments.** Don't suck it up. Fear grows bigger in the shadows, so bring all your insecurities into the light, where encouragement and grace live.

▸ **Calling out bravery in other moms.** Notice with intention how hard your tribe is working to love their littles with fierce truth and beauty. Point it out to them. Set aside comparison, jealousy, and judgment of other mama warriors. It is not brave to diminish a sister; it only makes us smaller too.

braver than you know

What are two ways in which your children have made you braver? How have they called forth courage in you that you did not know existed?

1 ....
....
....
....
....
....
....

2 ....
....
....
....
....
....
....

slowing down

Take this space to reflect on the areas in which you'd like to be a braver parent. What is the Spirit of God whispering to you? Nothing is too big or small. You are a warrior. What is your cry right now?

2

surrender

For all the difficult moments in motherhood
—the exhaustion, the depletion, the weariness and wondering—I think
the hardest part is letting go.

Letting go of what we think a particular season should be like. Letting go of what we think a particular moment should look like. Somebody along the way sold us on the idea that we were in control of these small humans. That snapping our fingers or directing the smiles on the Christmas card photograph or drying tears with soothing reassurances (however flimsy or false) gave us a certain amount of perceived control, as if we could make any moment okay in our children's lives and prevent the ones that weren't.

All the mommy marketing has supported this since the dawn of time.

Moms just make everything better. Crisis? Call your mom. Burned the turkey? Mom can help. Somebody broke your heart? Mom will know

Crisis?
Call your mom.

Burned the turkey?
Mom can help.

Somebody broke your heart?
Mom will know what to say
and which kind of carbohydrate
or chocolate to retrieve from the kitchen.

As Charlie and Pepper grow, they are experiencing
pain I cannot fix and outcomes I cannot control.

---

what to say and which kind of carbohydrate or chocolate to retrieve from the kitchen.

Maybe all of that sounds like a dated description of motherhood—maybe it is—but the heart of it remains true. Moms have always held our hearts carefully in one hand and a big box of Band-Aids in the other.

As Charlie and Pepper grow, they are experiencing pain I cannot fix and outcomes I cannot control. The pain that divorce leaves in its choppy wake. The pain of a second-grade crush unreciprocated. The embarrassment of tripping and falling down in front of that crush. The coach who has a different idea about who should be benched and who should play. The occasional lonely panic of preadolescence. The moments that can't be bubble wrapped or solved with warm chocolate chip cookies the way they once were.

I'm pausing here, in gratitude, as I ponder what that list looks like for other moms, lists that shame mine: Childhood cancer. The discovery of sexual abuse. Sending a hungry tummy to bed . . . again . . . because there is nothing left to eat. Hurts that don't need Band-Aids; they need triage and transfusions.

One afternoon when I was about six months into my strange new life as a single parent, I took the kids for a long walk under the gray Oklahoma sky. Pepper was only two and still happiest bouncing along in the baby jogger, watching the dogs and daisies go by, and Charlie was a fireball of a seven-year-old who needed to burn as much energy as possible to prevent physical implosion. So we headed out on an adventure off the beaten path.

I have always prided myself on being a person who is mostly prepared for all possible situations and outcomes. I have never been the mommy in the airport who ran out of Cheerios or diapers when the flight was delayed another six hours. I am the person who starts handing out my surplus to the other moms. I am a Girl Scout like that. I don't like surprises, and I am rarely unprepared for one.

But as we were walking that day, in an open rural area and far from our house or any other, I looked up and noticed the sky quickly darkening. I was new to Oklahoma and uninitiated by its storms. The wind began to pick up, and although I was armed with only a couple of juice boxes and some Goldfish crackers, I was trying to practice my steady, chipper mom voice so that my concern and fear would not betray me to my kids, who were still happily oblivious. To be clear, the main thing I felt was dread.

My panic was rooted solely in how afraid my children were. *I couldn't help them.* I couldn't make the rain stop.

Within a minute or two, the heavens opened, as I feared they would. We had no place to go. Nowhere. We were caught in a heavy, unrelenting downpour—to this day, the heaviest I've experienced in my life. Not a gentle pitter-patter. A straight-up wall of water and wind.

There was not a single tree large enough to stand under. We were utterly exposed. The wind would have rolled its eyes at my umbrella, had I been in possession of one.

Pepper was wide-eyed in the baby jogger, not crying, but stunned by the amount of water coming down. Her chubby little fingers acted as steady windshield wipers, trying to clear her own vision in front of her. I took off running with the stroller in the direction of our neighborhood (still so away), and Charlie ran beside me.

The rain came down harder and harder, to the point of absurdity. Intellectually, I knew that a mother and her two small children were not going to die in a rainstorm, but my panic was rooted solely in how afraid my children were. I couldn't help them. I couldn't make the rain stop. I couldn't even hear myself yelling to them that it would be okay.

At some point, my own anxiety overtook me, and I paused for a second to catch my breath. My feeling of helplessness took the wheel for a moment, and I stood there and started to cry.

They were tears for the scary moment that I could not make safe and happy. Tears for my scary life that I could not make safe and happy. Tears for all the storms. Tears for the end of a painful marriage. Tears for the uncertainty of my children's emotional health through it all. Tears for the unknown. Tears because I am the mother, and making things okay is my main job. But we were not okay.

I collected myself after a few seconds, and as we forged ahead through the tsunami in what I believed was the direction of home, suddenly Charlie took off running ahead of me. Sprinting, actually. It was so unlike him. He is a deep well of wonder, but he is not what I would describe as a free spirit. He does not do adventure without carefully weighing the pros and cons. He does safe and responsible. He is a firstborn through and through. A worrier. He is like me.

I was yelling after him, the wind carrying my voice up and away.

"Charlie! Slow down! What are you doing?!"

He's terrified, I thought. *He's trying to run home, but he doesn't know how to get there, and I can't keep up with him.*

Suddenly, Charlie spun around and faced me with the most beautiful smile I have ever seen on his perfect face, put both fists in the air, looked up at the punishing rain, and yelled, "We *surrender*! We *surrender*! We *SURRENDERRRRRR*!"

He was spinning in circles, laughing and yelling the words over and over again with double fist pumps in the air.

I caught my breath and followed his lead through my big gulps of tears. "We surrender! We surrender!"

I could hear Pepper squealing with delight from the stroller, "We 'render! 'Render, 'render!"

It was pure joy. We were shivering and scared and soaked to the bone . . . and fully surrendered.

We see you, storm. And we are okay. And we still know how to boogie and yell.

It is perhaps my favorite memory of motherhood.

Unprepared.

Unarmed.

Unbroken.

The student, not the teacher.

I don't remember when or how we got home and dried off. I don't remember the hot chocolate I likely made after. I don't remember whatever dorky mom wisdom I probably tried to impart once we were snuggled up.

I only remember the storm and the surrender. The thrill of letting go.

♡

letting go

Living a life of surrender means:

▸ <u>Lowering the bar.</u> I know this sounds strange since we are always striving—striving to be better, stronger, smarter, nicer, prettier, more patient, more perfect moms. But I cannot live with open, surrendered hands if they are clutching other things, including the measuring stick I use to gauge my performance.

▸ <u>Loosening your grip.</u> Sometimes I start my day by visualizing its events: The regular stuff. The chores. The errands. A flight. And then maybe the more meaningful stuff—lunch with a friend, a birthday gathering, a meal I made for a brand-new mom. And as I am lying in my bed, cursing the alarm and mentally rehearsing my day before it's begun, I slowly open my hands and say this to God: "If nothing goes as planned, I like Your plan better." I essentially admit to God and to myself that the likelihood of my controlling every detail is laughable. I know the curveballs are coming, and I'm okay with not being in charge.

▸ Trusting the source of peace. In every scenario that seems as though it is unraveling before me, instead of panicking and clamoring for more control, I ask myself this simple question: *What is the worst-case scenario here?* The kids are late to school? We reschedule the dentist appointment? We have to bring the friend takeout instead of homemade? I have to fix the crack in the windshield? The answer is usually not cause for crisis. And even if the worst-case scenario feels dire—the diagnosis is serious or scary or there's still no money in the bank—if I'm already living palms up and open in surrender, I'm ready to believe the words of Jesus: "I have told you these things, so that in me you may have peace. In this world you will have trouble. But take heart! I have overcome the world" (John 16:33 NIV). I can expect to find peace in the downpour.

▸ Remembering little ones are watching. I try to remember (because I really can forget) that my children are watching how I respond to life's big and little storms. When they're watching me unravel and dissolve into fear, panic, or stress the second the wind picks up, I'm quietly teaching them how to manage their own storms. Sure, I may tell my kids to put their trust in God and point to Scripture and a story to support this, but if they watch me grasping to control the uncontrollable, they might wonder at times how trustworthy God really is.

the storm and the surrender

If someone asked your children to describe how you handle storms, what would their honest answer be?

....

....

....

....

....

....

....

Can you think of a time when your child has been the teacher and you the student? What can you learn from kids' simple, uncomplicated belief that everything is going to be okay, from their own open hands of surrender?

....

....

....

....

....

....

....

....

slowing down

Take a moment and list the things you feel the most responsible for. The things that bring you the most stress and pressure. The things that would fall apart if you weren't in charge.

Now close your eyes and imagine writing them on the palms of your hands in black ink. Cover your palms with these worries and words—all of them. When you've finished, squeeze both of your hands into tight fists. Hold them there for a minute until you become aware of how hard it becomes to maintain that kind of tension. Now hold those fists high above your head and slowly open them. Imagine that all of the words now have wings, like butterflies, and they are flying one by one, higher and higher, until they are out of sight. Then lower your hands to notice your palms are free of writing. Ready to give and not clutch, ready to receive and protect. Ready to surrender. Thank God for holding in His hands what you were never meant to.

3

ring of fire

Charlie turned thirteen last summer. I am usually a
little emotional any time my kids are blowing out candles on a birthday
cake, but something about entering the teen years with my firstborn hit
me really hard. The natural separations had already begun: a little less
physical affection toward me in general, certainly, in front of peers. A
little more time alone in his room. A little less forthcoming and specific
with details of his school and social life. All things that signal the natural
maturing of a preteen. All things pointing to healthy independence and
development. All things that make me want to curl up in a ball and weep
for the boy who needs me a little less each day, as he is supposed to. We are
working hard to raise our children to be independent. We are mourning
the fruit of our labor.

One thing I've found challenging in these nearly teen days with
Charlie is finding a new way to talk about difficult or delicate things. He is

We are working hard
to raise our children
to be independent.

*We are mourning
the fruit of our labor.*

a raging introvert, like his mother. And like his mother, he spends a lot of time in his head and isn't overly verbal or communicative, to say the least. He is a deep well—sensitive, intuitive, and profoundly bright. His younger sister has never had an unexpressed thought or met a stranger, but Charlie can live on an island at times, making it hard to reach his shores.

I am discovering that an enormous part of parenting well means constant adjustment. Perpetual tweaking of my own expectations and hopes for my children. Trusting that when I don't think they are listening, they are still hearing. When they aren't really watching, they are still seeing. Finding new tools of communication and connection when the old ones are rusty and need to be retired from the belt.

When Charlie was three or four years old and I wanted to have a serious talk about something, I would sit him down on the couch and just start talking, eyeball to eyeball, about the importance of kindness, why lying is bad for your heart, having more patience, listening and obeying the first time. Charlie would clasp his chubby little hands together in his lap, nodding and listening carefully, occasionally adding his own adorable observations or additional confessions. Remember that wonderful age when your children would tattle on themselves?

I am discovering that an enormous part of parenting well means *constant* adjustment.

"How was your day at school, buddy?"

"Welp! It was great! But I made a couple of *real* bad choices at recess, so that stinks. And then I got in trouble again for talking too much in

To ask my thirteen-year-old to sit down with me on a couch for a lengthy, *meaningful,* one-on-one conversation would be like inviting him to have a root canal.

library time, so I had to sit in time-out, which still happens a lot. But it was mostly a great day!"

Charlie would ask a lot of questions on the couch. If I was being corrective, he was always sorry, always tender, always quick with monkey hugs and sloppy kisses. There were always closure and forgiveness and promises to try harder. Then he'd bounce off the couch and onto the next thing. He was never prone to tantrums or meltdowns; he was always very present and open, even at such a young age.

Some things about that time and those years made me drunk with exhaustion, but the way Charlie and I could talk together was one of my favorite parts.

It's so much harder now.

To ask my thirteen-year-old to sit down with me on a couch for a lengthy, meaningful, one-on-one conversation would be like inviting him to have a root canal. Hands shoved deep in pockets. One-word answers. Kicking around imaginary things on the floor. Eyes averted. Not disrespectfully, mind you. But that kind of conversation, even if it's not contentious or corrective, feels like torture to him. In my head I can hear Ward Cleaver's voice, in defense of an exasperated June, "You will look at your mother when she's talking to you, son!"

I've made the mistake of forcing this. Waiting out the dreadfully long and awkward silences until at least there is an exasperated reply to my satisfaction. It doesn't work.

It just doesn't.

I had a conversation about this recently with my friend Paul. When Paul married the love of his life, he also opened his heart and his arms to her amazing son. Nathan doesn't have any kind of meaningful relationship with his biological father, and building a relationship with Paul was a slow and beautiful process. Two steps forward, three steps back. The careful construction of trust. About the time Nathan hit the preteen years, the conversations got trickier because, bless their hormonal hearts, teens' whole lives are trickier. Paul told me that when it was time to talk about anything hard or deep or just plain awkward, they headed outside to the fire pit he'd built in the backyard.

The fire pit, Paul told me, allows them to *do* something while they talk. This is essentially how he explained it to me:

We have to gather the wood. We have to arrange it properly. We have to consider the direction of the wind and how to fan the flame. We're doing other things, which allows us to talk about stuff without the pressure of eye contact or silence or expectations. We each have to contribute to building the fire, giving us a little grace and margin within the spaces where words don't live. Even when the fire is raging and we've pulled up our benches around it, we can still focus on the flame while we're talking. Stoke it. Throw another log on.

Chat about girls. Grades. Friends. Pressure. We can sit and stare at the fire, and not at each other. It takes up the space where discomfort otherwise lives.

How simple and smart is that?

This conversation with Paul was a game changer for me. It makes so much sense. I know there will be another time in Charlie's life when we can talk more easily and directly, but for now I'm learning how to play video games and shoot a basketball in the driveway (it's as embarrassing as you're imagining) so we can talk about the hard stuff of life in the spaces between. On his terms, in his time—not mine.

creating connection

Connecting with my kids in meaningful ways means:

▸ Really listening to what's beneath my kids' words. It's so much more important to me to understand what their hearts are trying to say if they are having trouble articulating or explaining. This, of course, looks different with every age. Instead of "What's wrong?" or "What happened?" sometimes it helps to ask feeling questions: "Do you feel frustrated?" "Do you feel jealous?" "Are you feeling overwhelmed?" Questions that are aimed at excavating emotions and not just gathering information can go a long way toward understanding.

▸ Not forcing it. Children are not robots. We don't get to program their responses. Sometimes if my children don't feel like talking or sharing, I have to remind myself that they have that right and choice. Especially during the teen years, when they feel pressure on so many fronts, I want to be a sanctuary—a safe place where they can unravel or be still or ask questions, not another source of pressure.

▸ Declaring a shame-free zone. Designate a consistent time or place for family discussion. My friend Gina is raising three teenage boys, God bless her. They have designated Friday night as pizza night and "ask anything" night. And I mean *anything*. Her boys are invited to come with any questions, concerns, confusion, and confession and leave it all on the table every Friday night. It's a shame-free zone—nothing is off-limits. She says their questions (relating to sex, especially) have nearly made her choke on her pizza. It's given her a lot of insight into what the boys are picking up and learning from their peers at school, but it has also given her and her husband a chance to respond with truth and clarity as parents. Less lecture, more listening.

q & a

AMY GRANT, GRAMMY AND GMA DOVE
AWARD-WINNING SINGER-SONGWRITER

As your kids and stepkids have grown, what do you think is the secret to honest, healthy communication? What's worked, and what hasn't, when hard conversations are on the line? Any advice for young moms who aren't at that stage yet?

One thing I've learned is just to make yourself available to be in the kids' presence. Honestly, the kitchen is where this happens the most for me. Whether it is while I'm cooking dinner or doing dishes, being in the kitchen tends to invite the company of my children. Those who don't live at home will stop by to see what's on the stove. Our youngest, Corrina, will sit at the island and do homework.

In those moments, I try not to control the conversation or ask a lot of questions. Instead, I just listen and try to prompt more conversation from them by just being present. If I start asking questions, they tend to shut down. But if I busy myself with piddling around in the kitchen, acting almost disinterested, I've been surprised at where those conversations have gone and how much they will share. (The same kind of nonchalant conversation can be had over a ping-pong table, driving in the car, playing a card game, or sitting around a fire.)

Another thing I have tried not to do is to react too harshly to things I don't want to hear from them. Whether it is confessional about something in their own lives or if they are frustrated with me, I try to listen and welcome what they have to say with very little immediate reaction. Sometimes listening and observing without instant judgment is the best gift we can give to them.

Above and beyond anything, be respectful of your children when you communicate with them. You cannot demand respect from your children unless you extend respect to them.

talking points

Think about the times when your children seem most open to talking about difficult things. How can you protect and encourage those spaces?

....
....
....
....
....
....
....
....

What are some "fire pit" activities that might create a more relaxed environment for communication? What can you and your kids do together (fishing, hiking, cooking, drawing) that would help create easy, natural space for conversation?

....
....
....
....
....
....
....
....

slowing down

Think about your relationships—your friendships, family, or marriage. Timing is everything. When do you feel most open to talking about the hard stuff? Do you think intentionally about timing or another person's emotional space before you jump in with your own words?

_____

_____

_____

_____

_____

_____

_____

_____

_____

_____

_____

_____

_____

_____

_____

_____

_____

_____

_____

_____

_____

_____

_____

4

cheating on santa

One of the ways we utterly sabotage moments and memories with our children is by trying to micromanage them. We control and shape and orchestrate everything until a "moment" has become a manipulation. We love to blame Pinterest and Instagram for this pressure. I don't buy it. I mean, I'm as guilty as the next person who labors too long over the perfect filter to make my risotto look creamier, my Christmas tree more sparkly, and my crow's-feet awash in a beautiful blur.

We control and shape and orchestrate everything until a *"moment"* has become a *manipulation*.

But come on. The reign of social media did not create this pressure in our lives. It only threw gasoline on it. Those of us who have obsessed over the pages of magazines (remember those?) and idolized our favorite celebrity

TV moms (remember them?) can reluctantly admit that at the heart of the mommy-comparison game is our own inadequacy. Ask your mother or your grandmother if Instagram is to blame for this phenomenon. Watch her throw back her beautiful head of gray hair and laugh. The struggle is not new.

I'm realizing how many moments of real life I have sacrificed on the altar of perfection.

Even a simple and sweet commitment to a family tradition has left me susceptible to this pressure. For years we visited the same Santa at the mall. He is kind of legendary. By day he is a philosophy professor at a prestigious university, but one day someone keenly pointed out his remarkable resemblance to Saint Nick, and now every December he leaves his job on a college campus to let our precious babies sit on his red-velvet lap and whisper their wishes. The beard is real. The dainty

But this is our Santa! All the Santa pictures have to match the other Santa picture from year to year! *It's worth it.* It's worth it!

glasses, the belly, the chuckle—all real. The dreadful line around the mall to see him is *really* real. The first time my friend Shannon and I waited in line for multiple hours and I finally placed my baby in his arms, I actually started crying. I believed in Santa again for one beautiful, magical second. All our Santa pictures, every Christmas, were with this Santa. But as his popularity grew, so did the unfathomably long lines to see him. Shannon and I suffered through. We stood and paced

I'm realizing how many moments of *real life* I have sacrificed on the *altar of perfection.*

and jostled each other's babies and chased around our exhausted toddlers, stuffed in their cardigans and taffeta, melting down as multiple naptimes came and went.

This is our Santa! We are waiting in this line!

We ran out of snacks. We ran out of clever games to keep the kids occupied. We ran out of compassion for other mothers and their terrible, awful children who did not deserve presents. We ran out of the capacity to make rational decisions. We took Santa's name in vain under our breath. We wondered aloud if reindeer meat tasted like chicken.

But this is our Santa! All the Santa pictures have to match the other Santa pictures from year to year! It's worth it. It's worth it!

Most of the things we become **hyper-obsessed** about don't even register with our children as significant.

One year Shannon looked at me with fresh snot and Cheetos stains on her shirt and drew a line in the snow. "Never again. I'm never standing in this line again. There are other Santas."

And with that, we were finished with the only actual Christmas tradition I'd ever committed to keeping with my kids—until years later when I was held hostage by the daily shame that is the Elf on the Shelf.

We cheated on Santa. We saw other Santas. The pictures don't match—I'm not even sure where the pictures are now—but my kids never noticed the difference. In fact, most of the things we become hyper-obsessed about don't even register with our children as significant.

One year, for Charlie's tenth birthday, I made a campground in

> Was I ridiculous to go through all the effort? *No.* But was all that effort what made the memories so happy? *Nope.* Would I do it again? *Probably.*

our living room. I went to Home Depot and purchased actual pieces of *lumber* and drill bits called dowels or something and made seven different makeshift tents, a pretend fire in the middle with orange and yellow tissue paper flames, and a Mason jar lantern for each tent with its own battery-operated votive candle.

I don't think you understand. I can barely hang a picture on the wall. But five hours of YouTube tutorials later, I was building tents with power tools. It was beyond fun, to be honest. Really, it was. It nearly killed me, but I had such a blast with the whole thing.

What does Charlie remember about my Herculean efforts to create the perfect indoor Campapalooza? His friend Logan farting in everyone's tent until the boys almost lost consciousness from laughing. *Great.* Oh, and the pizza, which was delivery, and the only thing under my roof that wasn't homemade.

Was I ridiculous to go through all the effort? No. It was how I loved Charlie well on his birthday. But was all that effort what made the memories so happy? Nope. Would I do it again? Probably.

It's easy for me to look back at this and gently pat my former mommy self on the head. It's so different now. It's not that I don't care about "the moment" as much. It's just that I don't need to be the curator and hostess of my life. I'm not a museum guide . . . *If you'll look over here to the*

left, you'll notice all the Santa photographs that match *and the adorable birthday tents.*

My friend Shauna Niequist said it beautifully in her brilliant book *Present Over Perfect*: "Sink deeply into the world as it stands. . . . This is where life is, not in some imaginary, photo-shopped dreamland. Here. Now. You, just as you are. Me, just as I am. . . . Perfect has nothing on truly, completely, wide-eyed, open-souled present."

Slowing down doesn't always mean addressing external pressures, schedules, or situations. Oftentimes it involves taking a look at internal expectations. Slowing down our own selves long enough to notice that the guy who works at Jiffy Lube is a pretty decent Santa and Pizza Hut still has the best crust. *Open-souled present.* It means recognizing that the big, toothy smile on your child's face is never proportionate to the effort you exerted or your own ludicrous, self-imposed standards.

stop the performance loop

Really living in the moment with my kids means not just tolerating imperfection, but sometimes choosing it. If I want to recognize and fix my pattern of trying to create and control a perfect moment for my children, it means sometimes deciding to do some mediocre things. It means a small and simple birthday dinner. Staying home for spring break instead of trying to cobble together some trip I can't afford. It means store-bought. It is not my job to create every experience. I would rather be a part of them. That's where the real memories are made.

choosing average

In what parts of your life could you "choose average" once in a while to break the habit of curating and showcasing your child's life through your own parenting performance? What's the biggest offender?

....

....

....

....

What would it feel like not to care so much about the making of the moment and to be more present in the moment?

....

....

....

....

slowing down

Nothing is more soul-exposing than being a mom. It is the ultimate mirror, and it reveals the deep, hard stuff inside us that God longs to illuminate. Think about your own childhood for a few moments. Are there ways in which you overcompensate with your children as a reaction to old wounds that need healing or stories that need to be told?

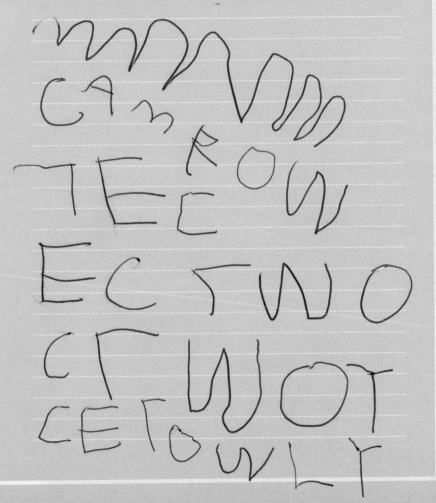

5

pour your heart out

My mom is not overly sentimental when it comes to childhood keepsakes. She grew up in a military family, relocating every few years when her father was assigned to a new Air Force base. At an early age, she was well versed in new schools and new friends and, having watched her parents pack and move so often, learned not to hang on to "stuff." Her life was spent separating the necessities from everything else. So, instinctively, Mom didn't keep items from my childhood—a decision she regrets now because of my incredulity about it. *I mean, not a single teddy bear or pair of baby socks.*

Conversely, one of my best friends kept half of the first Cheerio her oldest child ever tried to gum to death as a toddler.

I fall somewhere in the middle of the continuum of saving nothing and saving everything. I never caught the scrapbooking bug. It felt like something I would enjoy for three months and then it would become some guilt-laden albatross, like every fitness class I've ever signed up for.

Can we just pause here to acknowledge that this is okay? I wasn't sure for a while. If I hadn't had babies and toddlers before Pinterest and mommy blogs, I think I would have cratered under the expectations, even more than I did. I just decided early on to do what worked for me and not to waste too much soul-sucking energy comparing my parenting style to anyone else's.

For Charlie's first birthday party, I had not slept in one entire year because he was still so miserable with his reflux issues. I wore the same stained T-shirt for twelve full months. I absolutely could not summon the strength to throw the kind of birthday party I wanted (or was expected) to. I invited our closest friends and their kids to sit around the pool at our apartment on a sweltering Texas evening in July. I ordered pizza and got store-bought cupcakes. I know you can't even look at me right now, dear reader. It's okay.

Charlie wore a cute birthday hat and made a mess of his cupcake, on cue, but most of the photos of my son's first birthday involve friends jumping off a diving board and dads eating pizza. You're welcome, son.

(I've since made up for this moment in the party department aplenty.)

I kept the one-year candle from Charlie's cupcake. I did do *that* much. I've carefully stored the baby items that I think would be meaningful to my kids when they are parents one day: maybe not half-eaten Cheerios, but locks of hair from first haircuts, baby blankets, favorite books, the tiny knit hat they send home with the baby from the hospital. I kept Charlie's first stuffed animal, which was nearly attached to his body at all times. It was a gift—some combination of a cow and a giraffe we affectionately called Cowraffe. It lives in a box somewhere, waiting to walk down memory lane someday.

I was pretty diligent about preserving Charlie's keepsakes. It's possible that I might have slipped a tad in that department with Pepper.

Just last night I almost had a nervous breakdown. True story. For eight years I had carried around a memory card from an old digital camera that contains all the pictures from Pepper's first year of life. First days at the hospital, first weeks at home, first everything—a full year's worth. I've never gotten around to printing these pictures and putting them in her "first year" album, the way I did with her older brother. I just kept looking at this memory card, thinking, *I've got to do that soon.* Eight years, people. (Look away again if you need to.) It is my only photographic evidence of Pepper's first year of life.

Who doesn't print baby photos for *eight years?*
Who let this lady have children?!

I had put the memory card in a teapot, up high in a kitchen cabinet. I knew I would remember it there so it wouldn't get lost in a sea of pencils and paper clips in some desk drawer. I don't drink tea, so I don't even know why I own this vessel, but it had housed the memory card for a while.

Last night the kids had some friends over. I was in the next room working and heard Pepper say, "Emma! I'll make you some tea!" And then, like in a dream sequence, the slow sound of running water. In an instant, I knew what she had done, unintentionally, of course. I ran toward the kitchen like the slo-mo bullets in *The Matrix* to find my memory card drowning at the bottom of the teapot.

No. NO. Nonononononononononooooooooooo.

I raced up the stairs with the memory card. Patting it. Blowing on it. Encouraging it. Believing in it. Anointing it with oil. I had to dig out an old computer from storage because this memory card is so ancient, it isn't compatible with any device we use. I was trying to fight the tears.

Maybe it's a blankie or a lovey or whatever your family calls it, but it's *nonnegotiable*. It is the answer to every nap or tantrum or road trip.

Who doesn't print baby photos for eight years? *Who let this lady have children?!* Forty-five unbearable minutes later, the pictures were miraculously all still there, and that's when I let the tears come. "Thank You, thank You, thank You," I breathed.

Pepper's first stuffed animal was an elephant named Ellie. It was as sacred as Cowraffe—drooled on and hugged and dragged around to tatters. After a couple of years, I considered putting on a hazmat suit every time I picked it up to put in the washer. I know you know what I'm talking about—maybe it's a blankie or a lovey or whatever your family calls it, but it's nonnegotiable. It is the answer to every nap or tantrum or road trip. Ellie was loved to pieces, literally.

And then one day we lost it.

I don't know how or when or where, but suddenly the elephant was gone. On a plane, on a tour bus, in a restaurant, who knows? There's no replacing such a thing, of course, and eventually Pepper's tears dried, but I'm not sure mine ever quite did. I wanted Ellie to live in the box with Cowraffe forever. *This was Pepper's first best friend! What kind of mom loses her child's first and favorite stuffed animal?*

It can still really bother me when I think about it.

Moving into a new home recently forced me to go through all the boxes and bins of the memories and keepsakes I've saved from the early years of my kids' lives. I was in purge mode, as most of us are when moving day draws near. I was also going through a bit of a minimalist phase, taking serious inventory of how much unnecessary clutter and junk are in my home. I hadn't really considered that sentimental stuff counts as junk. How could memories and keepsakes be clutter?

Going through boxes of kindergarten drawings and gymnastics certificates and karate belts, I realized that hanging on to so much of that stuff was my way of trying to freeze time. Like if I can hold this cheap birthday princess tiara in my hand, it is proof that I once had a three-year-old. Proof that she twirled and laughed and made everyone raise their pinky fingers to eat cupcakes the way proper princesses do. It was evidence of sweeter, simpler times. And while the excavation of these trinkets made my heart swell, it also made me realize how easy it could be to live back there. To resent anything tricky or hard about the present because the past is so whitewashed.

Holding on too tightly to relics and memorabilia can fool me into

Holding on *too tightly* to relics and memorabilia can *fool me* into remembering things inaccurately. Everything was *beautiful* and *easy.* The babies slept soundly beneath the moon. I pureed organic carrots. *What?* Not even close.

remembering things inaccurately. Everything was beautiful and easy. The babies slept soundly beneath the moon. I pureed organic carrots. *What?* Not even close.

In the end, it was hard to part with a lot of the items that I thought I was so attached to because of the memories they represented. But I felt lighter and freer with less stuff in those boxes. It freed up a little real estate in my heart too—to be more present and less wistful about days gone by.

The most beautiful memories cannot be contained in a box in the garage or attic. They are etched into my heart forever, whether or not I can hold them in my hand.

what to keep

Deciding to be selective about the things I save or the things I don't has been freeing. I ask myself questions like:

+ *Why does this matter to me?*
+ *Will it mean something to me in the future?*
+ *Does it actually represent the moment I want to remember?*
+ *Will it mean something to my kids someday?*

If I can answer those questions honestly and still tuck the item in a memory box, I feel good. If I just start shoving second-grade spelling tests into storage, I'm not preserving anything, just creating more stuff to sort through later.

keepsake strategy

What's your current keepsake strategy? Lots? Little?

Do you feel pressure to preserve things you'd rather not? Do you feel pressure to memorialize moments with things?

slowing down

Do you ever reminisce about a certain age or stage of your child's life in a way that revises your own history or your child's? Why is that? Why might you look back with fuzzy rose-colored glasses but forward with stark, harsh reality? How can you choose not to manipulate a memory?

6

be the herd you want to see in the world

The deep and abiding love that Pepper had for elephants as a baby continues eight years later. Even now, they adorn her bedroom walls, dressers, T-shirts, and jewelry boxes. These creatures are gentle, deliberate, and kind. Slow and steady. Deeply tribal. Pep's personality better resembles an orangutan. Hopelessly silly with boundless energy, she's swinging from things most of the time. I find it kind of hilarious that she's decided her spirit animal is a creature as tranquil as the elephant.

One thing I've learned after countless television shows and elephant book reports is how village-oriented these elegant animals are—fiercely loyal and protective of their own. A friend of mine once sent me a picture of a herd of mama elephants in a circle with their backs to the center and tusks facing out. Another mama was in the middle of this circle, giving birth, recovering from an injury, or vulnerable in some way. This was her tribe's way of both protecting her and sending a message to any hyenas who might be thinking about making unwise advances in such a moment.

The image has long stayed with me.

Is this not the great gift we offer one another as moms? I have been both at the center of that circle and on the protective outer ring of it. Why on earth we waste one single minute feeling competitive with or critical of one another is beyond me. Let me tell you this: when you or your child is in trouble, the absolute last thing you will care about is your differences in discipline styles, vaccinations, commitment to organic vegetables, or the virtues of breast milk versus formula. You will care only about the circle. You will whisper your endless gratitude for that herd.

It took me a while to understand this, especially as new mom navigating through so much insecurity and uncertainty.

I was a newlywed in a brand-new city, who'd hardly had time to make any friends—and then suddenly an unplanned pregnancy. There were only a few women I actually knew at my baby shower. The rest were just people from church who graciously came so I'd have some version of a shower experience. I had no herd, no tribe at first. I felt as if I was flying solo trying to figure out this new role as mommy. Flying and failing and falling.

For some moms, it is simply second nature to be in community. You know who you are. You've had the same friends since seventh grade. You take girl trips to fun places. Your kids refer to all your friends as "Aunt" because they've been in their lives forever. You've never not been part of a tribe.

Why on *earth* we waste one single minute feeling *competitive* with or *critical* of one another is beyond me.

But for the rest of us introverts at home with babies, it is not that easy. The inside of your home is your sanctuary. You don't like leaving it. You resist and decline playdates because they feel like pressure to be someone you're really not. They also feel like a silent performance review, depending on how your kids behave. You are slow to ask for help. You don't do MOPS (Mothers of Preschoolers) or yoga or Bible study groups because you're not sure how to be both a mommy and an actual woman, independent of spit-up

It took a long time to finally succumb to the love of a tribe. *To let a handful of other moms encircle me.* Cry with me. Celebrate with me.

stains on your shirt. It's safer by yourself. No one can see how little you know what you're doing.

Does that description resonate?

No? Just me? Cool.

It took a long time to finally succumb to the love of a tribe. To let a handful of other moms encircle me. Cry with me. Celebrate with me. Hold my littles. Let me hold theirs. Slowly I realized we were trunk to tail, ambling along as elephants do, moving carefully and tenderly with one another through the unknown parts of this wilderness. It was the greatest gift I have known. I couldn't have survived those early years without the protection of a wise and gentle herd.

And although the landscape of my life has changed and my kids' needs have changed as they've aged, the importance of a tribe remains. I still have to fight my own instincts to be a recluse, to white-knuckle through

> It takes great strength to lay all your messiness
> in front of a tribe—**and tremendous trust.**

things alone. I still have to force myself to reach out and whisper in a tiny, apologetic voice, "Help, please?"

Modeling strength through vulnerability is my heart's cry these days. It takes great strength to lay all your messiness in front of a tribe—and tremendous trust.

Last year before Christmas, my dear friend Tiffany took Pepper to one of those pottery-painting places to paint something for me. Not surprisingly, Pepper chose a piece of pottery that depicted a mommy and a baby elephant, with trunks lovingly entwined. She painted tiny hearts all over both of them and told me I could hang my "special-est necklaces" on the tusks. Because Pepper wrapped it herself to put under the tree, she didn't know to consider how fragile the pottery was. Not knowing what the gift was, I also handled it too roughly a time or two, scooting gifts around to make room for others.

When I opened it on Christmas morning in front of my bouncing, beaming girl, we saw that one of the mama's tusks had broken off. Despite my gushing gratitude, I was certain I would see Pepper's lower lip start to tremble, so I rushed to assure her that we could glue it back on immediately and it would look exactly the same.

To my surprise, Pepper wasn't upset at all. She was incredibly proud of her artistry, shrugged off the broken tusk, and patted my back, saying, "It's okay, because their trunks are still wrapped around each other. The baby is still part of the mommy."

I swallowed a lump.

Indeed.

These are the achy moments we unknowingly sign up for.

The baby will always be part of the mommy. She will watch that mommy closely, paying attention to what she does with her weaknesses. Watching who she leans into. Noticing the protective circle that forms around the mommy during difficult times. She will learn the importance of support. She will find her own tribe someday because of what she's seen.

My tusks might break clean off a time or two. We will glue them back on and paint tiny hearts all over both of us.

Pepper was right. Her chipped elephant pottery is where I hang my most "special-est necklaces." The herd is where I hang my whole heart.

q & a

WITH **JESSICA TURNER**, AUTHOR OF
THE FRINGE HOURS: MAKING TIME FOR YOU

In what ways have you found the support of other moms to be the most helpful?

I often seek advice from women who are just ahead of me in the journey. I think sharing our wisdom with others is a gift, and I am always grateful for women who come alongside me. The Internet has also been a source of incredible support. From vulnerable blog posts to simple Facebook group discussions, I've been touched by so many moms online.

Have you ever been tempted to do it all solo because it was easier or didn't require as much vulnerability?

I think asking for help is difficult for most women. For years, I did not ask for help—both personally and professionally. I suffered because of my "I can do it all" attitude, as did my family and my work. Learning how to say, "Yes, I need help" brought me incredible freedom in my time and resources. Now I look for opportunities to ask for help!

What are the most practical ways you've found (in personal experience or through your blog or writing) in which women can "find a tribe"?

In my experience, I have found that investing in the community around you will reap the most rewards. While it takes work and intentionality, it is always worth it. For instance, my son has played soccer with the same kids for more than three years. The parents on his team have become some of our dearest friends. We have shared the highs and lows of life together.

And how can those of us who have an established herd reach out to the mamas in the margins?

Once a week, take a few minutes to reach out to someone you haven't talked to in a while. Let her know that she was on your mind, and ask if you can do anything to help her. Go a step further and invite her family over for dinner. If she doesn't live in your community, send her a card or an unexpected gift. These simple gestures of kindness go a long way in showing someone that she matters.

We need one another

Knowing that reaching out for support and community will never come naturally, I have to really commit to working at it. I have to force myself to step into the circle with honesty and humility. I have to say yes to the invitations. My friend Christa says there are two types of people: inviters and invitees. I am firmly in the second category, passively waiting for someone to include me, then unsure about participating.

But trying to do this mommy thing on your own—it's soul death. It might seem safer to stay inside alone, but isolation is so dangerous. God created and designed us to need one another.

your tribe

Who is in your current herd, if you have one? Are they people who are really for you and for your children?

Look around for moms on the fringes. Who can you pull into the circle? It's usually the one who looks as if she's got it all together on her own. Scratch below the surface, and you'll usually find a woman who desperately wants to belong somewhere but doesn't know how.

7

not at the dinner table

I remember pregnancy so well. Not the doctor's visits. Not the cold, blue gel spread thin over my enormous belly for the ultrasound appointments. Not the crib assembly, the tiny onesies, or the endless hours of stroller research. It's been so many years that I no longer remember the hours I spent buried in the pregnancy books and websites. Labor-breathing techniques. Baby names. Breast-feeding tips. The world's tiniest nail clippers. Those dreadful nose bulb syringes.

Mostly I remember lying awake at night, feeling a tiny fist or foot jabbing at my ribs, dreaming about life a little further down the road. I did not dream so much about swaddling and rocking and lullabies. There were endless beautiful baby memories, but for the most part, the infant years were very hard for me with both of my kids for different reasons. I dreamt more about the memories we would make as a family a bit later on.

I dreamt about the first magical moments I remembered when I was a little girl. I dreamt about gathering my kids around my kitchen table.

Some of my earliest, happiest memories are the ones my mom created around our table. In my mind, my own mother was made of glass. Perfection. An impossible memory to compete with or improve upon. Her own mother was largely unaffectionate, critical, and fairly selfish. Lost in

> Anywhere we gathered as a family and food was involved, it seemed *special* because Mom made it that way.

a sea of her own pain and dysfunction, she found parenting to be a chore and a bore and something to be endured. A friend of mine says that we approach our parenting either as a negative reaction or a positive response to our own family life and history. My mom reacted strongly, running in the other direction. No chance she would mother the way she had—or hadn't—been mothered. She threw herself wholly into loving my brother and me to the best of her ability—on any budget, no matter how challenging the circumstance, with bottomless love and generosity.

I have so many happy memories around the table when I was growing up. I've tried to remember why, exactly. It's not as though we were especially traditional. My dad did not walk in the door at 5:00 p.m. to a hot meal and well-behaved kids passing the green beans. Our schedules were busy and erratic. In addition to cultivating and sustaining home life, my mom was always very active and involved in life outside our home. We were on the go, like lots of families.

So my memories around a family table don't really fall into some category of wistful, sentimental, simpler times when Mom rounded the corner in slow motion, holding a steaming casserole. But anywhere we gathered as a family and food was involved, it seemed special because Mom made it that way.

I recently ran across a picture of my fifth birthday party. Me, with my bowl haircut in the middle of sweet little corduroy-clad friends wearing party hats. To my surprise, the table we were seated around was in a McDonald's.

Mom? *McDonald's?* For my birthday party?

When I asked my mom about it, she laughed and gently explained that once upon a time, parents didn't refinance their homes to throw their children a birthday party. There were no expectations of pony rides and bounce houses. McDonald's was cheap and what we could afford. We all got some little Mayor McCheese party favors, and I blew out candles on a cake my mom had made from a box mix.

I stared at the picture and at how happy I was. The table might have belonged to Ronald McDonald, but it was my table on my big day.

Another favorite memory from around the table was when our family sponsored two sisters from Brazil. They were attending a nearby Bible

We might not have been able to communicate with one another very well, but in savoring the flavors of someone else's well-seasoned traditions, our *hearts* (and waistlines) expanded. I'd never *loved* our family table more.

college where my mom worked, and my parents agreed to house them for a year, easing their financial burden and helping them find their way in a new culture. I was probably ten years old at the time.

The girls' English was rough. Our Portuguese was nonexistent, but those sisters were fluent in food. Many nights my mom let them take over, and our kitchen became a of flurry of unfamiliar smells, sizzling meats, and bubbling soups with strange but spectacular new flavors. I would watch in wonder, waiting expectantly for someone to ask me to stir something or knead dough. My mom taught the girls some of her own specialties, dishes that were more traditionally American.

Creating a table with **joy at the center** has very little to do with what's being served.

The sisters brought to our table all the energy and excitement they had experienced around their own native stove an ocean away. We might not have been able to communicate with one another very well, but in savoring the flavors of someone else's well-seasoned traditions, our hearts (and waistlines) expanded. I'd never loved our family table more.

Another favorite table was my maternal grandma Kiki's. I went to college in San Diego and lived just about thirty minutes from my grandparents. Kiki was a legend in the kitchen. My grandparents lived in Europe for many years, and when they returned, Kiki brought Paris home, tied up in her apron. Eating at her table was always extravagant, no matter how simple the dish.

So, on Kiki's birthday during my freshman year of college, I decided

> That table became the *center of our lives* at home. Obviously, we served and shared meals arount it. Stories too. Birthday candles were blown out. Crafts were glued. Glitter was spilled. Flour was scattered and dough rolled out.

to cook her dinner. At her house, of course—as I did not envision us gathering in my dorm room. I would handle everything, I assured her. I shopped and bought flowers and balloons. Then I boiled some water for noodles, opened a can of Ragu spaghetti sauce, and warmed up a loaf of garlic bread from the frozen-food department. *Ragu spaghetti sauce*—I actually did that in that woman's kitchen—with Kraft parmesan cheese shaken from the green jar. I was too scared to try anything else.

You would have thought I'd just won *Top Chef* by the look on her face after each bite. I think she used words like *delightful* and *exquisite* and made that furrowed-brow, closed-eyes expression every time her fork met her mouth. To this day, I cringe to think of it at all. And yet it's another favorite table memory of mine.

Kiki taught me, as did my mom and my Brazilian sisters and more than one McDonald's birthday, that creating a table with joy at the center has very little to do with what's being served.

After my divorce, the kids and I moved into a small rental house, where I would try to nurse my broken heart and, at the same time, attempt to forge ahead with some sense of normal family life for us. I bought really cheap "for now" furniture, including a square wooden table, not made out of actual wood, from a discount furniture warehouse. That table became the center of our lives at home. Obviously, we served and shared meals around it. Stories too. Birthday candles were blown out. Crafts were glued. Glitter was spilled. Flour was scattered and dough rolled out. It was the desk for homework, and occasionally a stand for my keyboard. At one point, we put up a portable ping-pong net in the middle of it and it became table tennis, literally.

And let me tell you, after year upon year of this kind of activity and abuse, the table was utterly trashed. I didn't care; I had paid next to noth-

---

This well-worn table was evidence of all the *love* that had been shared around it.

---

ing for it. And so when two-year-old Pepper colored on it with permanent marker, I didn't flinch. When I was giving myself a manicure and spilled a little nail polish remover, I didn't really rush to clean it up. The acetone instantly left a stain. I shrugged. For Thanksgiving I couldn't find a square tablecloth, so I covered the table with butcher paper and we scribbled our words and drawings of gratitude.

Even with the dings, stains, and chips in our table, I actually started to love it more. Each time I walked by it and noticed another flaw or scratch, my heart swelled because of the memory attached. This well-worn table was evidence of all the love that had been shared around it. I went from tolerating it as a "for now" piece of furniture to adoring it.

This is how I want my kids to remember any table we gather around— in our home, in a park, at the food court in the mall. I want them to feel every spill and scratch in their hearts as evidence of how they are loved and can show love, rather than memories of linen napkins and hands politely folded in laps.

I had to part with our kitchen table about six months ago.

I bought a house with a dining area that just couldn't accommodate the size and shape of the ugly, beloved table. *Besides*, I told myself, *it's time to buy grown-up furniture.* I let the table go with an ache and gratitude for every messy moment we'd lived around it. I blessed every stain and scratch.

After we moved, I purchased a nice "real" table, the kind you don't paint your nails on. When the furniture-delivery guys had finished setting it up, I was smitten. The new table looked so elegant and modern, and I could hardly wait to sit at it, sipping something fancy.

When the delivery guys left, I walked to one end of the table and noticed a pretty noticeable gouge in the wood that must have happened during transit. Right away I picked up my phone to call the company and begin the hassle of getting a replacement table as soon as possible.

But before anyone could answer, I hung up.

A dent before I'd even sat down. May it be the first of many.

kid confessions

SARA GROVES, SINGER-SONGWRITER AND RECORDING ARTIST

Of all the mundane and wonderful things that have happened at our table, the memory that first comes to mind is one of those late-night kid confessions.

My husband, Troy, and I were talking at the table after the kids were in bed. Toby came downstairs in tears and said he had heard an inappropriate joke at school and couldn't get it out of his head. Empathetic, we prayed for him, and for the kid that told the joke . . . and then Toby blurted out, "I'm the one who told the joke!"

Plot twist.

"Where did you hear it?"

We heard sniffles coming from the stairs.

"From Kirby!"

Our oldest son, Kirby, came around the corner crying. Both brothers were sitting across from us, waiting. Troy and I lectured for a minute, and I could tell both of us were trying to figure out that balance between "nip it in the bud" and "thanks for being honest."

Troy said, "You need to tell us the joke," and I knew that was it.

I put on my best Phylicia Rashad face, lips pursed: "Stand up and tell us this joke, and don't leave anything out."

There were squirming and tears, and embarrassment and long exhales, but they told the joke with all its color. It was a rare moment of parenting triumph because, clearly, telling the joke to us was the most fitting punishment ever.

As the boys went back upstairs, Troy leaned in to me and whispered, "That was . . . awesome!"

getting back to the table

The table is so sacred. Metaphorically. Literally. Kitchen tables. Picnic tables. Communion tables. Creating space to gather is really important to me. What's actually on the plates is not. Our table is central in our home and in our lives—so much happens around it and on it.

I've gotten in the bad habit of letting meals happen in front of the TV. Breakfast cereal on the couch, watching cartoons. Midday salad, catching up on CNN. It's easy to do. Or the car . . . ugh, *the car*. So many Chick-fil-A nuggets on the go.

I want to get back to the table—even if we're eating takeout. We can be eyeball to eyeball, fork to fork, with words, laughter, or even just ten minutes of conversation. Gathering and connecting matter so much. Those experiences will go a long way in shaping how my children gather around their own future tables.

table talk

What small changes could you make to coerce your family to sit around the table and really see each other for just a few minutes a day? If you have older kids, what "table jobs" could you give them to help encourage participation? Go outside and pick a flower to stick in a bud vase?

slowing down

Journal about any favorite memories you have around a table. Why were they special? How old were you? Why do you still remember these moments after so much time?

8

the best answer isn't always the right one

One of the most paralyzing parts of first becoming a new mom is the expectation that you will instinctively know what you are doing—right away. Once, after I expressed my anxiety about having my first baby, a man actually said to me, "Oh, please. Women have been squatting in fields and having babies for ages. You'll be fine."

This man is no longer in my contacts list.

It's kind of ridiculous, if you think about it objectively. It's your first day of a new job. You've had no training. No degree in this field. No supervisor. No experience. You drive your car into a parking lot lined with droves of excited family and friends, all holding banners and balloons and yelling advice and encouragement. But you walk in the door of your new job all by yourself.

And they hand you a baby—whether that child came from your own body or another brave sister entrusted you with hers—and you're just supposed to *know things*.

Years later, everybody will laugh about this, including you.

How terrified they were too. How little they understood. How panicked they were about the basics, even if they grew up with four siblings and had a Red Cross babysitting certificate.

Panic.

But the unspoken rule at your new job is not to show panic. Just keep smiling, use the word *blessing* as often as possible, and learn to do your job really well on two and a half hours of sleep. Then people will say you are a natural. Born to do this.

I know everyone has different new-mom experiences, so I'm not trying to project mine onto yours. Maybe you *were* a natural. I had a friend who could breast-feed and vacuum at the same time. She also didn't own a microwave because—*shrug*—who needs a microwave? I wanted to sneak into her house while she slept and locate the computer chip that was planted in her brain. She wasn't at all smug about her awesomeness—she was an incredibly loving and supportive friend, and she was truly just . . . a natural. Usually, after a morning dose of antidepressants, I was able to admire her with more ease.

My point is this: most of us have no idea what we're doing. *Still.* It's

Motherhood is the only course in the university of life in which you are expected to both *teach it* and *learn it* at the exact same time.

the great secret new moms don't know. And I think it's kind of a cruel secret because they would feel so much better about all that insecurity and angst and exhaustion if everyone else stopped acting as if they've discovered an essential oil that cures terror.

I am obnoxious around new moms now. In stores. At the park. On planes, especially. I basically assault them with affirmation: "Listen. I've been watching you, and you are doing a seriously amazing job. I mean, you're killing it. I wish when I had an infant I was half the mom you are."

Occasionally, I never make it past "I've been watching you . . ." before the mom starts to create some safe distance.

Motherhood is the only course in the university of life in which you are expected to both teach it and learn it at the exact same time. And the harder we try to fake our way through motherhood, the harder we make it on ourselves.

One of the biggest ways I have learned to be a more present mom is to acknowledge my constant student status with my kids.

Somewhere in the history of all the wonderful mom wisdom that's come before us, we have bought into the great myth that "I don't know" is not an acceptable answer, or, at the very least, a last resort. When you are a brand-new mom, "I don't know" usually translates shamefully and internally to *I know I should know. Why don't I know? Everyone else knows.*

When I was really struggling to breast-feed, one day a sweet new friend brought over her breast pump since I didn't have one. She brought

me a sandwich and a latte, unpacked the pump, and laid all the pieces in front of me.

> **Me**: Great. Thank you so much. This will really help, I'm sure.
> **Her**: Of course! Happy to help! You know how to use it?
> **Me**: Oh, well, yes . . . I do. I do know how. It seems very self- . . . Yes, I've got it.
> *(Standing in awkward silence for a few minutes)*
> **Her**: You have no idea how to work this, do you?
> **Me** *(committed to my pride)*: What? Yes! I mean, it's a breast pump, not a carburetor! I've got it.
> **Her** *(standing there compassionately)*: Keep eating your sandwich, and I'll just do it.

And with that, I let my newish friend (who is now one of my best friends) shove me into that contraption while I ate pimento cheese and cried a little from the embarrassment.

Why did I expect myself to know anything?

Now, smack in the middle of my son's preteen years, I'm realizing that I still fight the same internal embarrassment on topics I should be owning at this point: Online safety. Puberty. Video game ratings.

I can't tell you the number of times, even now, when I am carefully comparing notes with another mom, and one of us lets our guard down, revealing that we might not be experts in any given field, and instantly, the other nearly passes out from an exhale of relief. "Oh, *thank you* for saying that. I thought I was the only one who had no idea about that."

Immediately, the playing field is leveled. Wisdom is shared. Encouragement takes root.

The secret, new moms, is that you never really wake up one day with all the answers. It would be wonderful if childbirth or adoption classes would include an entire session on learning how to say, "I don't know." We could practice saying it out loud many, many times, and then maybe your spouse or your mom or a supportive friend could practice saying back to you, "Me neither."

This could go a long way with our little ones in the honesty department too.

We are so afraid that our children will question our authority or crumble underneath the weight of doubt if we aren't the experts on everything. How will they sleep at night if they suspect we are not omniscient?

The secret is that you **never** really
wake up one day with all the answers.

My take (after years of making up plausible but flimsy explanations) is that your kids will sleep really well because they value your honesty more than your vast knowledge.

In most matters of academia, you will give yourself away by the time you have a fifth grader. He or she will know you don't know a bunch of stuff, so don't even try. At the spelling bee last week, the very bright son of a friend of mine was eliminated on the word *burglarious*. Excuse me? I tried to look up the definition but couldn't because . . . *spelling*.

But in matters of faith, this gets slippery.

Both of my kids have always been very inquisitive and intuitive. And unfortunately for me, they can smell a tidy, fraudulent answer a mile away.

Charlie, at age six, asked at bedtime, "Mommy, how can God the Dad, Jesus the Son, and the Holy Spirit the nice ghost all be one, but separate?"

"Sssshhhhh. Night night, buddy. I'm gonna put your VeggieTales CD on."

Saying "I don't know" gives me more space to be an actual human, not a Wikimamapedia, and it gives my kids more room to lean into the mysteries of God.

"But how—"

"Okay. Night night, love. Enough talking. Ssssshhhh."

What?! How is this tiny child asking me to explain the Trinity at bedtime?

As my kids have gotten older, their questions have gotten more complicated. About God. About Scripture and religion. About science. About politics. About racism. About sexual orientation. About my feelings and beliefs about all those things.

Sometimes I have answers that come from firm convictions, and it's easy to share them. I pat myself on the back afterward, certain I've helped shape their worldview in an informed, compassionate, honest way.

But other times I have learned to take a deep breath and say, "I just don't know. I know as much as I think I know. I know what my life experience has taught me. I put my trust in God, who is holy and worthy of my trust. But if you're asking me for a 1,000 percent for-sure answer, I do not have one for that. But let's never stop asking God to show us truth."

Saying "I don't know" gives me more space to be an actual human, not a Wikimamapedia, and it gives my kids more room to lean into the mysteries of God.

So lean into the way your faith can deepen when you still feel safe enough to fall asleep without the Trinity making any logical sense, but trusting in a Creator who designed you to ask thoughtful, probing questions in order to know Him and love His creation better.

To have a heart that chases after truth, and the truth beneath that truth . . . and not the easy answer.

To be a student of life, at every age, about everything, and to recognize that God puts people in our path to teach us with their lives, and not just their smarts.

To value honest inquiry over rehearsed and scripted explanations.

To trust that at the end of every day, "I don't know" is a perfectly acceptable answer because knowing is not the end game and God's ways are higher than our ways.

q&a

WITH **NATALIE GRANT**, GMA DOVE
AWARD-WINNING SINGER-SONGWRITER

Of your three girls, who is the most inquisitive?

They are all pretty inquisitive, but Gracie is definitely the most. She has a constant, beautiful desire to know more. Her twin sister, Bella, is also quite curious, but she's fine letting Gracie take the risk to ask the tough stuff, and then she leans in to listen. And the youngest, Sadie, has plenty of questions, but she really likes to give answers! Right or wrong, that sweet little sugar and spice has an answer for everything.

How do you handle the toughest questions? Is there a quick story—poignant or funny—from one of the girls that involves a question you weren't sure you could answer?

It's amazing how young they start asking those tough questions, isn't it? I figured out pretty early on in my parenting journey that I was going to have to learn to be okay with sometimes saying, "I don't know." There is so much power and strength found in being vulnerable and transparent. I'm still on the journey of being consistent in that, especially as a mom. But I know that I have so often succumbed to the pressure of feeling like I always need to have the perfect and happy Christian answer—oftentimes saying what is rehearsed instead of just being honest. I want my girls to feel the freedom to ask questions and learn from a young age that sometimes there are just more questions than answers. But oftentimes the questions teach us more about real faith, believing without seeing.

When Gracie was six years old, I remember she asked why we can't see God. I tried to explain that our human eyes couldn't handle His power and greatness and that we'd have to wait for heaven. She continued, "But He could've made our human eyes so that we could handle it. He could have made Himself visible so that everyone would know He is real. Why didn't He?"

And with that, I just had to say, "I don't know." I told her that if we could see Him, it sure wouldn't take much faith to believe. But every relationship requires trust. And though I still had to say, "Baby, I don't know," the question led to honest dialogue and a beautiful conversation.

Now, at age ten, Gracie's questions are changing a bit: "Mom, why am I the only kid in our family who has to wear glasses?" "Why am I the only one in the family who has asthma?" "Why did God make my body look so different from my twin sister?"

Heart sink. Hold back the tears. Deep breath. "Baby, I don't know. But what I do know is that He's writing a beautiful story, and how He chooses to write it is always perfect, even when it seems confusing and hard to understand."

When we create space for the questions, uncertainties, and doubts, the dialogue is often what helps shape our faith. And I pray these open and honest conversations will help my children learn *how* to think about God, which is much more powerful than telling them *what* to think about God.

skilled living

Admitting my own ignorance and confusion or feelings of doubt and conflict (to the mirror and my littles) has been liberating. I've had to un-learn a lot of assumptions and expectations that I've absorbed over the years about what it means to be a responsible, confident, God-fearing mother. So much out there is supposed to be encouraging or equipping, and instead it's just more guilt in a pretty font.

The bar is too high . . . especially when we holler so much about be-ing a Proverbs 31 woman. I understand the heart and beauty behind that passage, but it has always significantly paralyzed me. It's a list of stuff you'd better know or else your kids will not only *not* rise up and call you blessed; they will probably rise up and go to juvenile detention in the eighth grade.

I'm on a journey. A journey involves dead ends and U-turns and the apology wave to other drivers (and occasionally an apology to the small people strapped into boosters in the backseat). How else will we model for our children the need for vulnerability and transparency if they do not first recognize the humility in us? Find me a well-adjusted adult who is just so grateful that his mom had *allllll* the answers, and I'll show you a nervous grown-up who is uncomfortable with even basic doubt: Parenting doubt. Faith doubt. Relationship doubt. We have to make it okay to ask and confess and do the clueless shrug.

> Skilled living gets its start in the Fear-of-God,
> insight into life from knowing a Holy God.
> —Proverbs 9:10 (THE MESSAGE)

Fearing God. Knowing God. This is the where we understand skilled living and insight. Not fearing the questions. Not fearing the answers that lead to more questions. Not knowing *about* a holy God. Knowing Him. On the honest dirt floor of life—where your kids want to sit anyway.

practice saying, "I don't know"

▶If you have very little ones: Practice saying, "I have no idea" in the moments when your mind is racing or scrambling for an easy, comfortable answer. Say it compassionately. Say it with all the humanity you can muster. Mostly, say it because it's true. Turn the question back to them: "What do you think?" Watch how important conversations are born out of sentences that don't end with decisive periods.

▶If you have older kids: Practice all the above, and also toss in an example of a time in your life when you really made a mistake in your decision making, thinking, or behavior. Talk about the implications, not to instill fear, but to confess imperfection and ultimately to communicate how loved they still are even when they have more questions than answers. Point them to truth and Scripture in a way that feels as if you are unrolling a road map before both of you. Make it less of a lecture and more learning together. Trace the directions and detours. Point out that the north, south, east, and west points of a compass look a little like a cross, where all roads can return.

slowing down

In what ways do you wish your mom could have been more honest about her questions and less rehearsed with her answers? How did this shape your faith and your parenting?

_____

_____

_____

_____

_____

_____

_____

_____

_____

_____

_____

_____

_____

_____

_____

_____

_____

_____

_____

_____

_____

_____

_____

_____

9

fixer-upper

My friends and I joke regularly that instead of setting up college funds for our children, we should set up therapy funds. I've sat on enough therapists' couches to know that when we are truly ready to start at the bottom floor of our emotional health, we start at the very beginning: The people who shaped us. The people who first loved or wounded us. The people who unknowingly paraded their own unhealthy habits right before us every morning over oatmeal and orange juice.

"Tell me about growing up."

"Tell me your earliest memory."

"Let's talk about your relationship with your mother."

I have done the painful excavation work myself. As an adult, I see my parents much more clearly. I have so much more admiration for the exceptional ways they loved me and a lot more compassion for the ways they got it wrong.

I cringe when I imagine either of my children as a grown-up, sitting on some therapist's couch, trying to identify and verbalize the moments I failed them and the scars or shrapnel I've left in his or her heart.

In this scenario, I usually picture myself popping out from behind the couch with snacks and elaborate explanations. "It's fine! *You're fine! Right?!* Let's go, sweetie. This is so silly." Also, in this scenario, I look amazing for being seventy.

Parenting is so hard. It's constant self-scrutiny. What am I clinging too tightly to? What am I holding too loosely? What I am ignoring? Overcompensating for? What am I justifying? Overlooking?

And maybe above all else, the question that runs as the strong current beneath so much of my parenting: *What else can I control?*

I grew up in a home that was very safe, very loving, and extremely supportive. No one ever raised his or her voice—ever. No doors ever slammed. My parents never uttered a harsh word between them or about each other.

That's not just my memory; that was actually how it was. My brother had some rough adolescent years. I navigated through the typical teenage moodiness, but I never remember my parents as anything but a perfect, kind, united, loving front—not in a creepy, Stepford way. They were just solid. And we were just an exceptionally healthy family.

When my own adult self landed on the therapist's couch, trying to understand why I have zero conflict-resolution skills and why I am hyper-averse to anything that smells even lightly of confrontation, I told the counselor about my wonderful family life, a version of the previous paragraph. I told him as if it were a badge of honor. How grateful I was to my

Above all else, the question that runs as the strong current beneath so much of my parenting: *What else can I control?*

folks for never exposing me to any conflict in our home and for shielding me from any unpleasantness.

Ahem.

One of the greatest challenges for me as a mom is allowing my children to **feel** their own **feelings**.

Bless the good therapists of the world, Lord. *Bless them.*

One of the greatest challenges for me as a mom is allowing my children to feel their own feelings. We are so hardwired to nurture and fix. To soothe and redirect and distract and chirp and pat and "there, there." Dads are strong and tough. Moms are soft. When our babies cry, we rock.

When our two-year-olds throw the spoon in frustration, we retrieve.

When our toddlers are maddened by falling towers of blocks, we rebuild.

When our kindergartners fall off the swing, we swoop in with Band-Aids and Popsicles.

When no one shows up at the lemonade stand, we text and beg friends and grandparents to drive by and act thirsty.

Second place in the spelling bee.

Missed free throws that would've won the game.

Forgotten lines in the school play.

The valentine that never came.

Fix. Fix. Fix. Soothe. Soothe. Soothe. Anything to prevent our children from feeling a twinge of disappointment or pain.

Can you imagine walking out to the lemonade stand and saying to your teary first grader who isn't having much luck selling drinks, "Sweetie, this is a good lesson if you're ever going to go into business for yourself. Life is hard. You gotta hustle, kid. Next time, bigger posters. Colder ice. Slash those prices. It's each man for himself, buddy. Now, let's get this cleaned up. I need my pitcher back."

I don't know—maybe you know moms who would actually give this real-life speech. Maybe you should unknow them.

So when does it stop? At what age do our children wake up and suddenly have to feel something hard?

A few months ago, I picked up Pepper from school, and we were walking back to the car. She was very upset because I was leaving the next day to travel for work. Tears upon tears were falling. I grabbed her hand and swung it in the air (as though we were about to start skipping) and began

---

We are so hardwired to nurture and fix. To soothe and redirect and distract and chirp and pat and "*there, there.*" Dads are strong and tough. Moms are soft.

---

to do my chirpy mommy routine about how the time would go really fast and I'd be back before she knew it. Then I actually heard these words come out of my mouth: "Besides, how sad could you be when we're going to get frozen custard right now?"

My seven-year-old stopped in her tracks. Tears streaming, Pepper dropped her backpack at her feet and pleaded through little sobs, "Mommy! Can you please just let me be sad right now?"

My own tears are welling up even as I remember it. I was *that* mom. The ice-cream-will-fix-the-heartache mom.

Something shifted in me that day. I suddenly realized that I could easily be that mom forever, and I would be handicapping my kids for life. They would have to fight even harder to have any normal coping skills when college applications were denied, jobs were lost, relationships ended, or a financial or health crisis hit.

I know plenty of adults who still have relationships like this with their moms. You probably do too. The relationship stopped growing and maturing at some point, when the children stopped needing their laundry folded and hot chocolate on cold days. They will always turn to Mom for comfort, but not much else. Certainly not direction or advice, and never with the hard stuff of life.

From the moment Pepper dropped her backpack in tears, I vowed to make some changes.

First, I recognized that my kids need to experience seeing my tears. I had never let them see my disappointment about anything. I had never let them see any cracks in my armor. It's what was modeled for me. My dad was Superman and my mom was Wonder Woman, and I was very lost and disillusioned when I finally figured out that they cried tears for their own failures and feelings behind closed doors.

One of the greatest gifts we can give our children is to be vulnerable with them. Not in a way that makes them fearful—they probably don't need to know if you're not sure how you'll pay the mortgage this month—but in a way that teaches them that great strength is found in transparency before God and one another.

> When I stopped seeing God solely as soother,
> easer of burdens, eraser of discomfort, I started
> to *trust* Him more in the valleys.

And I vowed to make vast space for my kids' own painful feelings when they surface.

I will let them experience brokenness without rushing to be their emotional glue. I will let them feel sad and sit with them in their sadness. I will allow anger and frustration. I will allow doors to slam and give space to cool. I will not rush in every time with advice or distraction or even hasty Scripture or prayer as anesthesia.

I will make our home a safe place for disappointment and fear and rage. And it will not be safe because I'm standing at the ready with a plate of cookies or a Bible verse. It will be safe because they can be their whole selves here. All of them.

So much like the gift God gives us as His children.

When I stopped seeing God solely as soother, easer of burdens, eraser of discomfort, I started to trust Him more in the valleys. Because God walks with us: Not running ahead, clearing away thorny branches or anything challenging from the path, and not whispering anecdotal feel-good sentiments to numb our broken hearts.

With us.

Present.

Sometimes in silence. Always with love.

stitches

PATSY CLAIRMONT, SPEAKER AND BESTSELLING AUTHOR

The nine-year age span between our boys didn't keep them from having big-time wrestling bouts. I pointed out to eight-year-old Jason that challenging his seventeen-year-old brother had its downfalls.

And downfall was the outcome during a body-slam attempt when Jason flipped over a footstool and cut his head open on the corner of the wall. My husband, Les, and I hustled him off to the emergency room.

Jason, shaken from the bump and wide-eyed at the sight of blood, asked, "How bad is it?"

The location of his injury was to our advantage because he couldn't see it. Somehow what we can't see doesn't seem as threatening.

"Not real bad," I assured him, as I mopped his injury while trying to apply light pressure.

"What are they going to do to me?"

Measuring my words, I responded, "Fix it."

"How?"

"They're going to put it back together again," I tried, hoping that would satisfy.

"How?" he pushed.

I'd run out of Humpty Dumpty stalls. So I went for the direct approach.

"They're going to stitch that gash shut," I declared.

He gasped. "Is it going to hurt?"

"Probably," I confessed.

"But what if it hurts more than I can bear?" he pleaded.

"Then you are going to reach down inside of you and pull up your courage. Jesus promised us we can do even hard things because He will give us strength. So if it starts to hurt more than you can bear, you pray, and He will help you."

Jason became very quiet. When we arrived at the emergency room, the doctor came in, looked at the injury, and began to prepare the wound for sutures. Before he began the stitching, he called in two nurses, one to stand on each side of Jason to hold him down when he began to flail.

Halfway through the procedure, the doctor realized the extra nurses were not necessary since Jason offered no resistance. Not once did Jason object, cry, or ask the doctor to stop.

One of the nurses was turning to leave when she noticed that someone else in the room was in need of help. I'm not sure if it was my jade skin tone or my side-to-side sway that alerted her, but she guided me to a chair and began to fan me. Later, the doctor assisted me to the car.

On the way out, the doctor said, "I cannot tell you what a privilege it was to work on a boy like that."

My husband shot me a glance as if to say, "Wish I could say the same for his green mother."

As we drove home, I asked Jason, "Did it hurt so bad that you had to pray?"

"Oh, Mom, I didn't wait. As soon as you told me, I prayed."

"What a good idea," I whispered. "I wish I would have thought of that."

raising resilient kids

Making space for my children's sadness or grief (or even basic disappointment) is one of the hardest things for me to do, and one of the most important. Because I remember my childhood as almost entirely conflict-free, I am just now really learning how pain can teach us. When I'm tempted to step in and immediately fix, soothe, or distract, I remind myself that I want to raise strong, resilient children who will be world-changers, voices for the voiceless, people with conviction and compassion. I'm not trying to release more thin-skinned people into the world.

In my house, when there are tears or slammed doors of frustration, I force myself to count to ten before I open my mouth. Not because I am trying to restrain anger, but because I am trying to keep myself from numbing feelings that need to be felt and spoken and wrestled with. I give myself permission to dry tears and rub backs without dismissing and fixing and saying a single word about ice cream.

messy feelings

How do you handle sadness in your home? How was it handled in your home when you were a child?

....

....

....

Do your children see you as a safe and secure place to *feel* and express their messy emotions or as a refuge where they run to feel better?

....

....

slowing down

We don't just get to slow down the good stuff. If we are intentional about being more present in day-to-day moments, that will always include the hard ones too. In what ways could you be deliberate about making more room for emotions that are not easily soothed? What strength could be born out of those moments, in you and in your kids?

_10_

the more things change

A fake magazine article purported to be from the 1950s still gets circulated quite a bit among women, as a joke really. "The Good Wife's Guide" is a point-by-point suggestion about how to keep your man happy from the moment he walks in the door from his stressful day until he lays his head down on the pillow at night. Here are just a couple of highlights from the article, but I encourage you to read it in its entirety when you really need a good laugh. It's easy to find online.

+ _Touch up your makeup, put a ribbon in your hair, and be fresh looking._
+ _At the time of his arrival, eliminate all noise of the washer, dryer, or vacuum._
+ _Try to encourage the children to be quiet._
+ _Caring for his comfort will provide you with immense personal satisfaction._
+ _Remember, his topics of conversation are more important than yours._

And my personal favorite:
+ _Arrange his pillow and offer to take off his shoes. Speak to him in a low, soothing and pleasant voice._

Um.

Let's just agree that I don't need to waste precious words on a page and you don't need to waste precious moments in your life reading how much the roles of marriage have changed, and how much women have gained in general, over the last sixty-plus years. It is both hilarious to read this article and depressing to think that an entire generation of women were raised to think that their husbands' happiness would be at the center of their fulfillment in life.

It is a **gross understatement** to say that a lot has changed for us girls. And we've got a long way to go.

I can get sad thinking about all the lost dreams. All the passion, calling, vision, innovation, and ideas that were suffocated under the blanket of cultural and social norms.

What did Grandma really *want*? In her *soul*? Or did she not feel permission to lie awake and ponder those kinds of questions? Did she resent making sure my grandpa's pillow was fluffed and taking off his shoes? While I never knew it, she did. Turns out, in addition to keeping an immaculate home and raising two beautiful, smart, and successful boys, my paternal grandma had to work odd jobs to keep the lights on because Grandpa's favorite activity was drinking scotch, which often interfered with providing for his family.

Of course, I had no idea.

To me, as a little girl, Grandpa was always such a gentle, big-hearted guy sitting in the recliner with his newspaper (and, evidently, scotch). All signs pointed to domestic bliss: Dust-free surfaces. Grandma's makeup was always "fresh looking." (Please see earlier chapters for any necessary reminders of pesky "silence and perfection" patterns in my family.)

So it is a gross understatement to say that a lot has changed for us girls. In the church. In our marriages. In our homes. In our careers. In our country. Hallelujah. And we've got a long way to go.

But here's the thing: plenty of things in the arena of motherhood have not changed. They are subtle and implied and damaging and very much alive and well.

I'm talking about the ever-celebrated virtue of busyness.

The lauding of selflessness.

The badge of coming in last place. Behind everyone. On purpose.

Giving away every last part of yourself to your children and their lives until you are a shell of a person who no longer recognizes her own reflection.

The most celebrated women are always the ones who are the *most exhausted*.

These are some of the hallmarks of being a good mom. Think about it for a second. When you hear the description of an amazing woman (whether it is at her birthday dinner, her promotion, or her Bible study), it almost always involves some version of, "*How* does she do it? She puts everyone first and still has more to give." The church is particularly guilty of this. The most celebrated women are always the ones who are the most exhausted. Time and time again we praise and honor women for putting themselves last in their lives. And we happily accept the accolades because they make us martyrs.

I've lost track of the number of times I've texted my friends with my mommy martyrdom. "Haven't showered in days and just did McDonald's drive-through for dinner . . . again. LOL #badmom"

To which my friend texts back, "You are an amazing mom!"

(Thank you.)

Or I meet people when I'm touring who say, "How do you *do* it? How do you balance the travel and the parenting and strike a healthy personal balance?"

"Basically, my only alone time is on the toilet, and I haven't had a pedicure since 2002. LOL!"

"Well, you are so wonderful for sacrificing to come and sing for us. It can't be easy!"

(Thank you.)

Mommy martyr. *Check*. And that puts a little wind in our sails.

How many times have you heard your girlfriends say, "All I want for Mother's Day is to go to a hotel by myself for twenty-four hours and read or sleep." As if isolation is the most extravagant or lavish gift our families could give us.

Friends, what are we doing?

How much distance have we actually gained from that ridiculous, fake 1950s article? Are we now replacing husbands with children? Pillows fluffed. Full attention. Profuse apologies for anything that resembles *self*-care, and not childcare.

Please hear me: *Your exhaustion is not the measure of your success.*

What are we saying to our kids when our entire lives revolve around them? Never before has our culture been so child-centric. We are apologizing constantly with our lives by ignoring our lives entirely. We're teaching our children that to love someone well, you must give no attention to yourself. Diminish. Shrink.

I took about ten years off from writing and recording music to stay at home. My manager nearly had a heart attack because I made this decision at the height of my music career, when a lot of people had worked very hard on my behalf and we were just starting to see the fruit of years of touring, promotion, and plain ole teamwork. And I just bailed. The truth is that my marriage was in shambles, and I had to step away to prove to myself and to my husband that family was first. It was crisis management.

But I let my fans and listeners think it was a mommy move. I didn't want to talk about the fact that my marriage was on life support, but I sure

"Haven't showered in days and just did McDonald's drive-through for dinner . . . *again*. LOL #badmom"

didn't mind the many articles that were written praising my decision to step out of the spotlight and into a full-time life of crushed Cheerios and juice boxes. Though I didn't orchestrate that kind of attention, it sure felt nice.

Wow. How sacrificial. She walked away from all that success and adoration because being a mommy is more important. Hats off to you, Nichole. God will honor this!

(Thank you.)

And while I would make the same decision all over again for the same reasons, I can easily recognize and confess how unhealthy it was that my martyrdom felt so affirmed by those voices.

And once the reality set in that I had completely reoriented my life around my children—abandoning my gifts, my calling, my passion, and my joy I felt in those areas (not believing I could have both)—I instantly struggled with resentment.

I would see a woman in the preschool drop-off line in her gym clothes, clearly headed to work out, and I would think. *Oh, must be nice.* I would read about my peers who were taking their kids on the road with a nanny on a tour bus, juggling it all, and I would stew. *Oh, must be nice.* I would hear about other moms (lots of them) who would get sitters so they could get their nails done, or join a book club, or get their master's degree, or open a yoga studio, or write a book. *Huh. Wonder what* that's *like,* I'd think. *Must be nice.*

What must be nice? Being an emotionally healthy person whose children are growing up to see a strong, whole woman living from the center of her God-given passion to do what she loves while still deeply caring for the little ones she loves?

This sounds counterintuitive to the idea of slowing down, doesn't it? But being a whole woman is at the very heart of it.

We can't possibly slow down enough to cherish the small, everyday, perfectly imperfect moments with our children if we are so committed to running ourselves into the ground in the hopes that someone will notice how sacrificially busy we are.

In the aftermath of Christmas morning, after everyone has run off to try on their new clothes and play with their new toys, have you ever

We can't possibly *slow down* enough to cherish the small, everyday, perfectly imperfect moments with our children if we are *so committed* to running ourselves into the ground in the hopes that someone will notice how sacrificially busy we are.

sat alone in the middle of a mountainous disaster of wrapping paper and felt simultaneously proud and sorry for yourself? Best Christmas ever, though. *Good job.*

If we are missing the joy of moments, we are missing the actual moments.

Can we collectively agree to lower the standards of creating experiences in favor of remembering and enjoying the experiences? *All* moms can do this. Office moms. Working-at-home moms. Student moms. Boss moms. New moms. Adoptive moms. Stepmoms. Empty-nester moms.

Do we really want our kids to describe us someday by our frenzied ability to control chaos? Do we want our eulogy to be about how small we made ourselves? Do we want people to remember us as women who made no time for our own needs because of the fear that we might be judged for making spiritual, physical, and emotional health a priority? Worst of all, are we accidentally raising egocentric, self-absorbed small humans in the name of selflessness in hopes that God is pleased?

In order to raise a strong woman, we have to be able to recognize one.

Expect a little pushback for your wonderfully confused children at first. You kinda created this. It will feel foreign to you and to them initially.

But you've got this.

Instead of trying to slow down time, slow down *you*. Do something for yourself today and every day. Then watch, in wonder, how everyone not only survives but thrives.

Dear twenty-six-year-old Penny,

Your husband is on his second combat tour in Vietnam and here you sit, nine months pregnant with your first baby. You're living alone in a tiny house in Victorville, California, scared to death. You know absolutely nothing about babies or even why you thought having one was a good idea. But today is the first day of the most wonderful journey you could never imagine. Without any significant modeling of what good parenting should look like, you will commit yourself to be a "perfect mother." That will be your first mistake, for failure surely looms around every corner. But your beautiful daughter is quite forgiving as you put the diaper on backwards (seriously!) and can't figure out how to burp her to save your life.

You will miraculously survive these early years. You will look back and not understand how. Your daughter will have awkward ballet lessons and endless piano recitals. You will pay soccer fees to watch her pick daisies in a field. There will be countless musical productions, which she, of course, will narrate and direct, and countless PTA meetings. You will be exhausted but extraordinarily fulfilled.

A full calendar of school activities will subside and make room for the angst of the teenage years. You will realize that there is plenty that "a perfect mother" cannot fix. Your daughter will have a boyfriend crisis, maybe two. There will be significant struggle as she strains to find herself. Take some time to let her express her feelings and disappointments—to her, they are very real and will significantly shape the young person she will become. That person will look very much like you, but for very different reasons.

You will spend decades trying to please everyone, at great expense to your own sense of self-worth. Your daughter will also become a "people pleaser," but for different reasons—her love language is giving. She will be generous to a fault with her time, resources, and emotions. She will give away so much of herself that there is nothing left for her. Take the time during her younger years to show her that her value lies in the person she is—her ideals, principles, and passions—not in what she does.

Both of your kids will be very active in their small Christian school, which they will later refer to as a cocoon. You will see it as a sanctuary where the school has to be the bad cop about clothes, rules, social mores. Penny, don't relinquish your responsibility and influence during this time. Plow through the challenges together. Your children will be stronger for it, and your relationships will thrive, certainly with the victories, but even in the losses. During these years, your daughter will teach you an amazing life lesson about forgiveness and mercy as you struggle with the death of your marriage. You will not model what you wish you could at times, which will cause some very rocky times in your relationships. Your children will begin to rebel and question when they realize that real life never happens in a cocoon.

You will be frantic as you watch everything you have so carefully orchestrated disintegrate seemingly overnight. You will be anxious in this uncharted territory. As frightened as you are, your kids will be terrified and looking to you for strength and stability. Don't try to be their best friend. They may appear to think that's "cool," but what they will want is to climb back into the safety of the womb. Let them know you understand—because you want to climb in with them!

Fast-forward to adult years. You will suffer with your daughter as she survives the death of her own marriage. She will continue to struggle under the weight of others' expectations but will make amazing choices for the future of her children. Glitter, glamour, and success will be at her fingertips, but she will quietly walk away. You will never be prouder of her. She will have finally broken the cycle—actually starting with your own mother—of needing to be valued by others at the expense of her own self-worth. Her children will be confident and focused and hold her in the highest regard.

You will enjoy one of the most fulfilling chapters of your life as you serve the Lord next to the partner whom He will so unexpectedly plop right down in the middle of your life. You will never have expected such joy and fulfillment.

God still has so many adventures planned for you, but don't be in such a hurry to discover and execute. Slow down.

say what you need

It took me a long time to acknowledge my own passive-aggressive tendencies. When I feel utterly underappreciated and overlooked, I am the queen of the obnoxiously heavy sigh. I invented it.

I have a black belt in heavy sighing when I am the only person who knows how to put a dish in the dishwasher. I'll put every dish away extra slowly to make sure everyone hears my very demonstrative displeasure. Guess who notices every single time?

Exactly nobody.

My current practice (which, ironically, is something I've been teaching my children since birth but can't manage myself) is just to say what I need.

No disclaimers. No apologies.

Pantene aired a commercial a few years ago called "Not Sorry." I have no idea how it helped them sell shampoo, but it's a solid thirty seconds of scenes in which women constantly apologize for no necessary reason—it's a natural, deferential posture for some of us. I could have starred in this commercial.

I'm still learning how to communicate clearly and kindly what my needs are. My kids do not look at me as if I have three heads. They usually nod and occasionally make a point to remember in the future, wanting to be a part of Team Happy Mom.

Nobody imagines that I am a better mom, human, or Christian when I have eliminated any personal need for joy from my life. God is not honored by my fatigue. But everybody feels a little lighter in our home when I remember to be nice to myself.

reclaiming space

What small things or moments would remind you that you have a self apart from your role as a mom (Short of booking a trip to Turks and Caicos)? Think of tangible, doable things that would help you reconnect with the parts of you that have been ignored, the parts you allowed to diminish and disappear over time. What could you do to reclaim those spaces inside you?

Have something in mind? Good. Take a deep breath. Don't apologize for being overwhelmed, tired, or selfish. Don't kick the dirt when you sheepishly ask for what you need. Just say it. Then do it.

slowing down

If this resonates with you, try to remember how and when you learned that being a mom who erases any need or self from her life is some sort of jewel in your crown. Was this modeled for you? Was it taught in the context of a woman's identity in the eyes of the church or the Bible? How you can unlearn it? Unteach it? Are there ways in which you feel proud and healthy about the boundaries you've drawn around your own self-care? What positive connections do you recognize in your own life when you've made your own emotional health a priority?

a little louder, please

I am counting on the fact that Pepper will not read this book until she's much older. Otherwise, I may have to hide any copies that end up in our house until we can all laugh about this subject matter.

Here are the facts: Pepper is eight years old and a hot fashion disaster right now. *Right now?* She has *always* been a fashion mess. I have never met a child who is more creative in how she expresses herself. Fashion is Pepper's current medium. I cannot begin to describe the outfit combinations she puts together. Mere words are insufficient. I would need to finger-paint something in neon and plaid and lace and glitter and rhinestones and animal prints and Crisco and Elmer's glue and spackle—and this would all be in the same painting.

My disclaimer here is that I am not a mom who sees this as a reflection of my own sense of style. Listen, I have a ton of emotional issues and plenty of parenting baggage, but thankfully projecting feminine perfection onto

Pepper's wardrobe is not one of them. She hasn't worn a matching outfit a day in her life. Not for family pictures, not for special school concerts, not to sing onstage with me in front of eight thousand women at a conference.

I credit my own mom with my healthy detachment from my daughter's sense of . . . um . . . style. I have heard my mom tell too many stories about my own special wardrobe choices growing up. When I was slightly older than Pepper, at age fifteen, my mom got to sit proudly through church mother-daughter luncheons with me donning black leather jackets,

Certainly dying a slow, internal death, Mom never batted an eye or uttered a word about my clothing choices to me.

raccoon-inspired kohl eyeliner, and clunky Doc Martens. Then she would slide behind the piano and accompany me as I would sing to a roomful of lace and ruffles. Certainly dying a slow, internal death, Mom never batted an eye or uttered a word about my clothing choices, which conveyed to me: *Be who you are. Dress however you feel you want to express your truest you.* (For the record, modesty was not something I ever challenged.)

A couple years later, when I was in high school, a good friend of mine and I decided we were fed up with the rules of fashion. "Who makes these rules?!" we demanded. We were also very philosophical about the amount of money these fashion rule makers decided we should spend in order to flaunt their stupid trends. We were very deep teenagers. We boycotted all the corporate things and shopped only at secondhand stores (before this was a desirable thing, dear hipsters), boasting about how many stained

Let's be honest, moms: we need our **wonderful** children to reflect back how **wonderful** we are. How hard we are trying, for Pete's sake. The loveliness we'd like to project. How *thoughtful* and *intentional* our parenting is.

shirts and broomstick skirts we could score under ten bucks. Our parents had plenty of money for normal, new clothes, and we attended a private school. But our trench coats were some sort of a statement to the people.

So that year I sang once more at the mother-daughter luncheons dressed in my "I am a privileged white teenager impersonating a gypsy backpacking across Europe" outfit. *Dare you to stare.*

My mom still supportively played the piano for me, unflinchingly, in her Talbots blazer and smart navy heels. She was proud of whoever I was, in whatever phase I was in. Period. *She also dared you to stare.*

I owe a lot to my mom for modeling this for me. It has enabled me to let Pepper walk out the door in cowboy boots with Easter dresses and go to church in gold metallic Converse shoes and blue sequined skirts. And please do not ask me to comment on the jewelry and hair accessories that are involved. I am not currently able.

I recognized a long time ago that Pepper's outfits are a very literal expression of her own amazing creativity. She's like a walking Picasso. The shapes don't always make sense together, and sometimes you have to look away for a second, but you know an authentic and real piece of art when it is present.

We always accuse dads of trying to mold their mini-me boys. Their sons have to love the sport they love, or play the sport they played, or cheer for the same team . . . the *only* team for which the men in the family have cheered for generations. But let's be honest, moms: we need our wonderful children to reflect back how wonderful we are. How hard we are trying, for Pete's sake. The loveliness we'd like to project. How thoughtful and intentional our parenting is.

Most of the time when I am really mortified by my children in public, it is because of the perceived judgment I feel from all the other moms around me. How many times have we apologized at a playdate, "I'm so sorry! He never acts this way at home! He must be so tired!"? Please. He acts this way every dang day. Or how many times have we chuckled under our breath and rolled our eyes apologetically because of what our children have decided to wear, certain someone is sizing up our own ability to discern hideously erroneous wardrobe combinations? "What are you gonna do?" We chuckle nervously. "Lost the clothing battle this morning!"

Instinctively, I decided to protect myself and started saying things loudly *to* my child but not really intended *for* my child. Have you done this much?

It's not about the other moms; it's about us. It's always about us. Our own stuff. Our own insecurities. Our own need for approval.

When Charlie was in preschool, I picked him up one day, and the kids had just finished playing dress-up. All the other preschoolers were putting away the firefighter hats, karate belts, and stethoscopes, and Charlie was sitting in the middle of the room wearing a pink princess dress, sobbing.

I went to him immediately, and the teacher tenderly explained that he *really, really, really* liked dressing up like a princess that day, and most decidedly did not want to take off the costume (clearly). He just sat there in a puddle of tears and taffeta, sobbing over and over again, "*I love being a princess!*"

Right away I was hyperaware of the self-consciousness and anxiety creeping up my neck, but not worried, mind you, about my actual child, who was inconsolable. All the other moms were in the room now, gathering backpacks and trying not to glance at the scene unfolding in the middle of the room. I felt exposed—and minor rage.

So, instinctively, I decided to protect myself and started saying things loudly *to* my child but not really intended *for* my child. Have you done this much?

"Buddy, you've never even worn a princess dress before! How silly! *It is time to take it off so we are not late for hockey lessons!*"

(In fairness, we *were* taking hockey lessons at the time, but it's a wonder I didn't make up something about elk hunting for added masculinity.)

I was so flustered and embarrassed, and I just kept coercing Charlie loudly for the sake of the other moms who were present. He started crying harder, of course, sensing no tenderness from his main person.

The preschool teacher, beautifully seasoned for moments like these, came over, knelt down, and said quietly, "Charlie, if it's okay with your mom, you can wear the princess dress home and bring it back tomorrow."

He looked for my approval through swollen eyes.

If we go through life apologizing with our words and posture and faces for parts of our children that embarrass us, when will that end? *It won't.*

My stomach sank. I felt so awful.

What was I doing? Who was I being? *Who are you, and what have you done with Charlie's mom? Where is his* main person?

I thanked his teacher with my eyes, scooped him up in that dress, and loudly announced that I had the perfect matching lip gloss at home. And I did.

Charlie wore the costume until bedtime. He was the most beautiful princess you've ever seen. And we danced and danced and I took him to Chili's for glamorous chicken tenders. And then the next day at school he put the dress back on the costume rack and went back to banging on drums and practicing for his next belt in karate. That was the end of it.

The lesson for me was not about being concerned about appropriate gender or identity roles, although my younger self would have been.

It was about seeing Charlie for Charlie, not as a reflection of my own insecurity. Seeing Pepper for herself, past her own fascinating wardrobe decisions, and not as a reflection of how unpolished my parenting is. We don't have permission to work out all our own junk on the beautiful blank canvases of our children, but that doesn't stop us from trying.

And if we go through life apologizing with our words and posture and faces for parts of our children that embarrass us, when will that end? It won't.

Their teen trouble will humiliate us.

Their failures will define us.

Their divorces will embarrass us.

Their unemployment will shame us.

Their sexuality will paralyze us.

Their politics will horrify us.

We will whisper in hushed tones about their depression and their addiction far, far, from the town square.

What will all of this say about us?

Practice now. *You are mine. You are God's. You are everything wonderful. You are perfect as you are. You are loved without condition. You make me proud every second of this day and every day after.*

Practice now, and practice loudly. Speak up so the judge-y, staring moms can hear you clearly.

♡

reset button

Surrendering to the embarrassment of a situation never gets easier. It wasn't easy with a sobbing boy in a princess dress, and it is not easy in sulky, preteen moments when I am mortified by open disrespect. *What. Did. You. Just.* Say?!

This sounds overly simple, but sometimes just quickly reminding myself in those moments that I do not answer to anyone else but the same loving Creator who wove together my children's beautiful DNA, and He can help me hit the reset button.

I don't answer to offended grandparents.

I don't answer to nosy strangers.

I don't answer to condescending, unsolicited comments.

And while I will always try and stay open to criticism and input from loving, trusted sources, ultimately, I answer to myself and to my God.

Also, the Princess Charlie episode taught me a hard lesson about never, ever shaming my child in an effort to make myself feel or look better. The temptation to do this is still strong. But the comments we make about our kids in front of others will last longer and louder in their little lives. No matter how embarrassed we are, let's protect their dignity—always. My kids should feel as emotionally safe with me when they publicly crash and burn as they do with me privately.

coping strategies

Can you remember a time when you were beyond embarrassed by your child? What sort of issues did it stir up that were more about you than about the actual situation or scene that unfolded?

....

....

....

....

....

....

....

....

What coping strategies for public meltdowns could be helpful for you and your kids?

....

....

....

....

....

....

....

....

....

....

....

slowing down

It's so natural to draw parallels between the way we love our children and the way God loves us. Sometimes it's the only real way to explain the depth and ache with which we adore our children. If that's the lens we love through, it might be worth considering the way God "handles" us when we embarrass ourselves. The way He gently corrects. The way He is still fiercely committed to adoring us. Dare you to stare, He says. That's My kid. How might this kind of grace inform the way you respond to those less-than-proud moments with your own children?

12

taking the "make" out of memories

Traditions are a funny thing. They can live in the minds and memories of families for entire generations, being carefully observed and handed down. Or they can be born the instant someone says the phrase, "Let's make this a tradition!"

I remember just a couple of traditions in my family when I was a little girl. We celebrated most things the regular suburban-American way. Traditional Thanksgiving. Cookies for Santa. A quarter under your pillow from the Tooth Fairy. (Someone please try and convince my children that she left only a quarter.)

But one tradition I loved dearly was how we would spend New Year's Eve with Grandma. She would have been visiting for Christmas most years, and right about the time December 31 rolled around, my parents were a teeny-tiny bit ready to get out of a house saturated with bored, snowed-in kids and one precious, though slightly uptight, grandma. My

---

We celebrated most things the regular
suburban-American way. Traditional Thanksgiving.
Cookies for Santa. A quarter under your pillow
from the tooth fairy.
(Someone please try and convince my children
that she left only a quarter.)

---

parents couldn't get dressed up to go out fast enough. I don't know where they went; they weren't the party type. They probably sat in that brown Oldsmobile in the driveway and drank champagne for a while. In silence.

My kids would describe my mom as a nut—probably the silliest Nana alive. When we are all together, we laugh until we are holding our sides and tears are streaming. There is much merriment in the kitchen. Lots of cooking and talking over one another. Massive eye rolling when Nana says something slightly clueless or naive, followed by more hysterical laughing. Nana and the kids would play endless hours of the Sorry! board game. It's basically the only game we own, and it only comes out when Nana visits. I love that my children will have memories like this with my mom. Our only complaint is that she lives too far away.

But that was not my experience with Grandma. I wouldn't describe Grandma as fun, necessarily. She was . . . how shall I say it? . . . reserved. She was immaculate about her entire life. Her hair literally never moved. Her nails were always filed to perfection. Her slacks were without a wrinkle or crease. She was not a "let loose" kind of grandma, but I utterly adored her. She was such a loving and supportive force in my life.

And God help the person who ever spoke ill of any of her grandchildren. Nobody was permitted to breathe a word of criticism about us. The same was true only for George W. Bush and Bill Gaither. I felt rather proud to be a part of this holy trinity.

So on New Year's Eve, when my parents went wherever they went to reclaim their sanity, our tradition was for my little brother and me to stay up late (presumably until midnight, if we could make it), sit on the floor in front of the nearly dead Christmas tree, play Monopoly, and eat peanut M&M's.

That's it. That was the whole tradition. Pretty exciting, right?

It was so hyped in my mind, it might as well have been Dick Clark in Times Square with cannons of confetti going off. I looked forward to it with disproportionate glee, considering what was actually involved.

Could we have played Monopoly any (or every) night of Grandma's visit had we wanted to? Of course! Was this the only time of the year we were permitted to eat peanut M&M's? Hardly. But somebody, at some point, uttered the word *tradition*, and it became magic every year. It's still magic in my memory.

These days we are so convinced that our children require extra-special everything. They don't. We require it for them. (I am holding Elf on the Shelf recovery classes, if anyone wants to participate. There will be back rubs and hugs.) Sometimes the only thing that turns an ordinary event into a special tradition is just calling it one.

These are some of our simple traditions over the years.

Going for frozen yogurt after the first day of school every year. We sit and talk about teachers and classes and friends, high and low points, fears and excitement.

Going to dinner at Tulsa's oldest, tackiest, most overly decorated restaurant around Christmastime and ordering the tableside Caesar salad. We did this one time, and then the next year my kids said, "Are we going to that beautiful Christmas restaurant for Caesar salad again this year? We have to! It's a tradition!" (It is? Okay, then! It is now!)

On Christmas Eve, we change into new pj's and slippers (including adults and any visiting grandparents). A limo pulls up in front of the house expecting a fancy group to get in, and we pile in with pillows and blankets and ask our driver to take us to see the best Christmas lights. Then

---

These traditions will be carved into my kids' hearts and memories **forever**. They are simple and small, and who knows why they are special to us, **but they are.**

---

we always ask him to stop at the Krispy Kreme drive-through because we think we are hilarious, and also we exist for donuts.

We usually try to spend the last weekend before school starts and the first weekend school is out for summer with the kids' cousin Tyler, who is also Charlie's best friend, from Oklahoma City. (Actually, Tyler has become a part of a lot of our traditions.)

For many years when the kids were very little, our Halloween tradition was to make Kraft Mac and Cheese and chili for dinner before trick-or-treating. Chili mac. What? Apparently, this is what their dad had done growing up, so we just continued it. To this day, on Halloween night, it feels like the right thing to eat.

Sometimes the only thing that
turns an *ordinary event* into a *special
tradition* is just calling it one.

When the kids were small, I would sneak in their bedrooms the mornings of their birthdays and take a picture of them right when they woke up, capturing the very first sleepy look of a sweet face one year older. (This tradition no longer continues, by the way. Thirteen-year-olds do not appreciate this, nor do they like to be woken from their slumber for any reason, let alone the cataclysmic devastation of being the subject of one photograph. Fair enough.)

That's the thing about traditions. We get so attached to preserving them that we struggle with letting them go when it's time to make some space for new ones.

Whenever we see my two goddaughters, all four of the kids have a Cheetos Puff–eating contest. It's exactly what you think it is: How many Cheetos Puffs can you stuff in your mouth? My jaw cramps thinking about it. But when we get together once or twice a year, the question is always, "Who's bringing the Puffs?"

These traditions will be carved into my kids' hearts and memories forever. They don't involve elaborate planning or preparation. They are not expensive (except for the limo). They are simple and small, and who knows why they are special to us, but they are.

I utterly expect full-grown kids to still be shoving Cheetos Puffs into their faces at one of their wedding receptions. We will be having that Caesar salad each Christmas as long as that old restaurant is still filling every inch of bare space with cheap, plastic poinsettias. In twenty years

I hope we're still tipping the limo driver extra to drive through Krispy Kreme.

Maybe we will be, and maybe we won't.

That's the other thing about traditions. We get so attached to preserving them that we struggle with letting them go when it's time to make some space for new ones. We don't always have to use Grandmother's fine china at Thanksgiving. Someday the Elf on the Shelf might actually just stay on a shelf somewhere (please, Moses and Mary, let it be). I lost the tiny homemade pillow where the kids put their teeth for the tooth fairy. It was the cutest and a favorite part of my own mommy traditions, but the fairy still came every time. And you'd better believe she left at least one dollar, or the earth would cease to rotate on its axis.

I think the key to really relishing these moments is to pay attention to the moments your kids think are special, even if they make no sense to you and don't seem worthy of a scrapbook page. We miss what's special about these traditions when we become too attached to pulling them off with poise and precision.

I'm telling you: Monopoly and M&M's.

Don't overthink it.

becoming halloween people

SHAUNA NIEQUIST, *NEW YORK TIMES* BESTSELLING
AUTHOR OF *PRESENT OVER PERFECT* AND *SAVOR*

My husband, Aaron, and I were never really Halloween people. We're not into zombies and tombstone decorations. We're not pumpkin enthusiasts. I'm not a fall person at all—not a "can't-wait-to-break-out-my-sweater-and-boots" person, not a pumpkin spice latte lover. We never boycotted Halloween. We never turned off our porch lights and hid inside, but we definitely didn't put cobwebs in our trees or fake spiders on our porch or skeletons holding machetes in our bushes.

At least, we didn't until two years ago.

Our son Henry is eight, and he is all imagination. For most of his life, he's been wearing costumes everywhere he goes—capes, masks, gloves, imaginary jet boots, power rings. We almost don't notice it anymore. Henry loves Halloween, and a couple of years ago he asked a few times if we could have decorations. We told him we're not really decoration people. We hoped he'd forget about it.

And then the day before Halloween, Henry started carrying things out onto the front porch—rubber snakes, pirate hats, fake swords.

"What are you doing, buddy?" I asked.

"I'm making it spooky," he said.

His face lit up with delight.

All afternoon Henry dragged things from his bedroom and the basement out into the front yard. He tied a fake lizard to the doorknob by its tail; he wound rubber snakes through the bushes; he hung capes in the trees.

At a certain point I called Aaron and said, "I give up. I think we need to go to the store and get this kid some spooky decorations. He's in his glory out there."

Aaron agreed. We woke Henry up early on the morning of Halloween, and we spent the morning setting up lights shaped like skulls, cobwebs with huge fake spiders, poison signs, and pumpkins.

Henry was beside himself.

When his friends came over to trick-or-treat, he proudly walked them around all the decorations, explaining each thing.

At the end of the day, after the chaos and candy eating was over, Aaron and I decided that we're Halloween people. We're Halloween people because Henry is a Halloween person, and more than anything, we're Henry people.

Loving Henry is loving spooky, scary stuff. Loving Henry is getting up on Halloween morning to spread fake cobwebs and line the driveways with lights shaped like skulls.

Sometimes love asks you to change.

This is a tiny example, certainly, but life is full of opportunities to love someone well by loving their thing, not just your thing, by stretching across your preferences and opinions and comforts.

It's so easy to love people who like all the same things you do— who never listen to music that makes you cringe or who believe all the same things you believe. But love sometimes asks you to lay down your preferences and dive into someone else's world for a little while.

Sometimes that world is full of fake spiders. Sometimes it's the ballet or country music or Russian novels. Sometimes it's staying quiet when you want to talk; sometimes it's giving space when you want to rush in. Love asks what's best for the person you love, not what's best or most convenient for you.

natural and meaningful

When I was growing up, our family didn't have many traditions. I have lots of wonderful memories, but not a lot that are rooted in generation after generation. I don't remember hearing stories about customs, rituals, or relics that were passed down and must be preserved.

Maybe that's why I am open to redefining the very word *tradition* for my kids. Any tradition we keep has to feel natural and meaningful, even if it's silly. The whole point of trying to slow down the holidays or special occasions is to sink down deep in the middle of the moment. Having a tradition, however small, sort of anchors that moment more in my memory.

new and old traditions

Do you have any favorite established family traditions? Why are they meaningful to you, and how did they begin?

....

....

....

What about starting some new traditions? Try letting your kids decide on a new a tradition or two this year—maybe it sticks, maybe it doesn't. But helping them pay attention to special (and everyday) moments is good practice for when they'll need to slow down someday. What are some possibilities?

....

....

....

slowing down

Which holidays or seasons feel the most rushed and chaotic for you? Which memories would you most like to slow down and pay closer attention to? What small things could you change about the way you celebrate that might help you feel more present? As a mom, do you feel responsible for creating every experience? Are there ways in which you might be able to excuse yourself from the ringmaster role so you could experience those moments too?

_____
_____
_____
_____
_____
_____
_____
_____
_____
_____
_____
_____
_____
_____
_____
_____
_____
_____
_____
_____
_____
_____
_____

practice makes practice

As I've mentioned previously, Pepper is passionate about personal expression and creativity—with her wardrobe and accessory choices, with crayons and scissors, and most recently in the kitchen. She is severely opposed to actually following recipes or listening to any instructions. She wants to make her own creations from scratch. I both love this and do not love this.

An average afternoon in the life of Pepper involves walking in the door after school, dropping her backpack near the front door, and marching straight into the kitchen, where a flurry ensues . . . opening cupboards and drawers, taking out measuring cups, spoons, spatulas, and whisks. While she feels particular pride in lining up all the kitchen utensils, she finds even more delight in lining up the ingredients for her creations.

I have a hole on the inside of my cheek where I have bitten or held my tongue in protest, all in the name of Pepper's creativity and self-expression.

A year ago it was condiments. Pepper was obsessed with mixing any and every combination of condiments she could find in the door of the fridge. She was committed to being impartial. Every condiment got to participate.

Behind Pepper's back, I named this recipe BARF. Here is the recipe for your enjoyment. Please print it out.

Ingredients:

- ketchup
- mustard
- Worcestershire sauce
- the juice of one lemon
- a dollop of sour cream
- some ranch dressing
- a tablespoon of maple syrup
- chocolate chips
- cat food
- a splash of Dr Pepper
- pickle juice
- food coloring
- paprika (fill in any spice here)
- salt and pepper

Stir the above ingredients in a large bowl. Throw away.

I can't stress how visually nasty this consistency was. Not one time did I ever taste even a tiny bit of this. I do not love my child that much.

> I have a hole on the inside of my cheek where I have bitten or held my tongue in protest, all in the name of Pepper's **creativity** and **self-expression**.

That was last year.

The current expression of Pepper's kitchen creativity is centered more around baking. She has learned the basic ingredients to make a cake—flour, sugar, eggs, milk, and so forth—but she is aggressively opposed to anyone pointing out the appropriate *amount* of each ingredient. She takes great joy in winging it.

This usually means either a half dozen eggs with a teaspoon of flour or four cups of flour with a splash of milk, hold the eggs. Pour into ungreased cake pans, and tell Mom how long to bake and at what temperature. If Pepper is worried the batter might be too thin, she freezes it instead of baking.

It was so cute the first forty-seven times, but I have needed jackhammers and chisels to remove this cake batter from its pans, bowls, and my counters, and I am over it.

The other day I gave Pepper a real cake batter recipe and armed her with all the items she'd need to pull off this delicious endeavor. I hoped that maybe baking something that didn't smell like gym socks in July might be exciting and empowering. It was torture.

She's never known such drudgery. Having Pepper to dutifully comply with some grown-up version of cake making was ghastly. She rolled her eyes and heavy-sighed the entire time.

So often I have to fight my instincts not to point out when Pepper is doing something the *"Wrong Way."* I'm smart enough to know this breaks down eventually.

My enthusiasm for the cake's sweet, golden fluffiness was not helpful. Pepper's sighs grew heavier. She was utterly unattached to (and even annoyed by) actual success and far more invested in the joy of the experiment.

Pepper is the utmost free spirit in every aspect of her life.

She went through a stage when she wanted to put stickers on every surface of her bedroom. What qualified as a sticker was anything that could stick to something. She peeled off price tags and SKU codes from grocery store items and stuck them on her wall. You know those bathing suit liners that come in new bathing suits in case people are gross enough to try them on without undergarments—the hygienic adhesive things that you peel off once you've purchased the item and taken it home? She stuck it on her door. Hey, you say panty liner, I say sticker. Tomato, tomahto.

So often I have to fight my instincts not to point out when Pepper is doing something the "wrong way." I'm smart enough to know this breaks down eventually. Algebra is not subjective. Biology does not care how you *feel* about cellular structure. It is what it is. No one is going to discover the cure for cancer by mixing nail polish remover and shaving cream and calling it "the healing ointment."

But the question I keep coming to over and over again in my parenting is, *So what?*

Why can't Pepper make ketchup barf surprise or cake batter with

The question I keep coming
to over and over again in my
parenting is, SO WHAT?

the consistency of a hockey puck? Why can't she stick panty liners on her closet door? Why can't she spend the afternoon planting dead Christmas tree branches in the soil, watering them, and waiting for a forest to grow?

She is just practicing. Not practicing for success, just practicing for practice's sake. Practicing what it feels like to be herself.

For the fun in failure.

For the sake of self-expression.

For her own self-confidence.

For the thrill of coloring outside the lines—or erasing them entirely.

I suddenly realized that this is exactly what I have modeled for Pepper by my own admiration of others; she comes by it honestly. I think about what I am drawn to creatively as an adult, and the truth is, I place great value on originality.

When I was in sixth grade and slaving away at weekly piano lessons, my teacher was endlessly frustrated. I adored her, but I hated practicing. I lacked discipline and motivation and, worst of all, I started inserting my own "flavor" and signature chords into the classics. Can you imagine? Getting to the very end of a perfect Bach composition, with all its complicated fingering precision and the sheer genius of its movement, and then tacking on your own ridiculous jazzy ending for the last few notes? My poor teacher went white every time. I'm queasy thinking about it. But the truth is, I was just flirting with songwriting. That was the beginning. And even though I still practiced Bach begrudgingly, that year I wrote my first-ever song and sang it in front of the whole school. I felt that "thing" happen in my young heart— when you're doing something you should be doing.

Not every mistake needs correcting. Not all embellishment and

interpretation need monitoring. Don't put up those ridiculous bowling bumper rails that ensure every child knocks a pin down. Let there be gutter balls.

Last week Charlie tried to make a machine that would dispense slime. He found a homemade slime recipe from an online tutorial, and for three days our table was covered in glue, Borax, and food dye. So much slime—we were a snail colony. Even though he always cleaned up, I wanted to scream at what a disaster it was.

Then Charlie tried to build a vending machine that would accept loose change and dispense a blob of slime. I do not even have the energy to describe the construction except to say it involved supergluing Jenga pieces together and dismantling an IKEA unit. I'm sorry, but who takes IKEA furniture *apart* once it's assembled? I knew from the first blueprint that the contraption wasn't going to work—it would never dispense slime. But I kept my mouth shut and enjoyed every moment of Charlie's determination and enthusiasm. All the hours of effort . . . none wasted. He was fine to abandon it eventually. He just had fun.

I still love songwriters who break the rules. I love poetry that doesn't rhyme. I love experimental chefs who push past the boundaries of predictability in their kitchens. I love modern art. I love pastors and spiritual directors who speak and lead the margins. I love irregular architecture. I love teachers who don't use textbooks. I love politicians who surprise me. I love doctors whose practices are unconventional. I love people who have stared down all those traditional rules and social norms and said, "No, thanks. I'm good."

And I love a good mistake.

Behind every truly original and innovative thinker lies a giant pile of accidents. Mess-ups. Do-overs. Failure is central to greatness—I believe that.

Behind every truly original and innovative thinker lies a giant pile of accidents. *Mess-ups. Do-overs.*

When we overexamine and overcorrect and control, we make the world smaller for our children by shrinking possibility and keeping imagination in check. So many beloved children's stories involve grown-ups who didn't get it, couldn't see it. Encased in their stodgy, gray grown-up worlds, they shook their heads and shushed the magic. Willy Wonka. Dr. Seuss. Narnia. Hogwarts. Little ones making wonderful, accidental, surprising mistakes in the face of disbelieving, dreary adult people and their world of rules.

Our children will know soon enough about this world. Why rush them toward reality so quickly?

I can't actually slow down time, but I want to see what my children see for as long as possible. I want to pull more ingredients off the shelf to go into mystery cake batter. I want to dig my hands in the soil to help plant the Christmas branch forest. I want to paper the walls with stickers and keep worms for pets and add snazzy jazz endings to Bach's masterpieces.

I want to want more wonder.

the beat of her own drum

ELLIE HOLCOMB,
GMA DOVE AWARD-WINNING SINGER-SONGWRITER

I was playing for an adoption benefit, and Emmylou, who had just turned three, kept asking if she could come sing a song onstage with me. I felt nervous about this for her, so I walked her through when and where she could come onstage to sing. We had a little stool set up for her in front of a microphone, and the plan was for her to sing the first song of the night with me. As I was introducing her and getting her set on the stool, Emmylou leaned toward the mic and said, "Actually, Mom, I'm gonna drum." My heart started beating really fast. This is not what we had planned. I was both a mom and an artist performing, and I had no idea how to handle the situation.

This was not going to be the sweet moment I pictured in my mind in which people would see that my daughter knows my songs and is learning the truths I've woven into them. I wanted to correct Emmylou and say, "No, baby . . . this isn't what we planned. You need to stick with what we said we were going to do." But it was too late. She had already climbed down from her stool. She had seen a smaller step stool as she was walking onstage, grabbed it, carried it behind the drums, and my precious drummer, Elizabeth Chan, handed her some soft mallets.

So I introduced the song. "Well, this isn't what we planned, but here comes Emmylou's debut on the drums as we play my song 'Broken Beautiful.'" I could barely get through the song because I could *not* stop laughing! My drummer kept perfect rhythm as my three-year-old enthusiastically *hammered* on the drums alongside her. When we finished the song, Emmylou came back around to the front of the stage and grabbed my hand to take a bow.

I was so glad that I didn't have time to let the "make sure your children look perfect because they are a reflection of you" tendencies in my heart stop her. I loved seeing her independence and confidence. I loved that we delivered a very imperfect performance of my song "Broken Beautiful." How fitting! And I especially loved that a whole crowd of people got to see me let my little girl literally march to the beat of her own drum. Ever since that night, Emmylou has referred to herself as a drummer. Now I think twice before I try to stop my kids from simply being themselves.

creative experiments

I remember when my kids were tiny, budding artists. It took me approximately three seconds to become the mom who hung every page of smeared and scribbled crayon onto my fridge. Each piece was perfect—genius! It went straight in the memory book when we needed room for new masterpieces on the fridge.

I want to treat my kids' creative experiments the same way now. Bigger kids make bigger messes, it's true. But someday I'll have a perfectly clean, project-free table and an experiment-free kitchen, and I will weep bitter tears. Every day I want to grab a magnet and hang stuff on my mental fridge—creative conversations, invention ideas, entrepreneurial dreams— letting my kids breathe without correction or suggestion for improvement.

relax your standards

What sort of "messes" could you reframe as your child actively practices creative expression? Can you find the same joy you felt when you hung up the scribbled crayon art? Could you speak with the same enthusiasm and affirmation?

....

....

....

In the art of slowing down, messes have to become less important. In what ways could you relax your standards a bit?

....

....

....

....

slowing down

What about the creativity in you? At some point, all of us finger-painted or made a sand castle or cut tiny paper shapes out of construction paper. Was there a point when you think you simply "outgrew" your creative side? What parts of your life or passions might still be hinting at a creative flame that never quite went out? Would you be willing to show yourself the same kind of encouragement you show your kids in an effort to coax out that gift again?

14

stones and swans

We used to live in a house near a pond. Pepper was only about three years old and home with me all day, every day. We walked and walked and walked around that pond. Sometimes we skipped or ran. We walked our dog. We fed the geese. Many days we sat on the bench and watched as a beautiful white swan would glide toward us as if on glass. For some reason, this swan seemed to love Pepper and would always paddle close to the shore when she was present.

One afternoon during one of our many pond adventures, Pepper was ambling along the path as the swan glided along nearby. My sweet girl stopped and sat down in the dirt and started to collect rocks. I watched curiously as she tried to stack them carefully on top of each other, becoming increasingly frustrated every time the stack fell down, to the point of tears. But she kept starting over. At some point I realized that she was trying to make a swan out of these little rocks, a tribute to her graceful friend.

She could not figure out how to make the swan's neck because it bends and curves in places that rocks cannot.

I knelt down and wiped a couple tears with my thumb and said sadly, "I'm sorry, baby. I guess stones can't be swans."

"Stones can't be swans, Mama," she repeated.

This is what a life of faith looks like to me sometimes. Longing for beauty. Longing to build something that resembles grace. Desperate to have something important and impressive to show with my handful of dirty stones and stacking them tall enough to be noticed by God. Watching them fall. Wiping tears. Starting to stack again. Recognizing my own limitations, but feeling the gaze of a loving Creator over my shoulder.

This can be especially true when I am trying to help shape the faith of my children. The pressure to get it right starts early. The fear of getting it wrong whispers persistently.

I remember reading a pop-up book of Old Testament heroes with Charlie when he was little. Pop-up David. Pop-up Moses. Pop-up Noah. Pop-up Lot. I remember wondering at the time, *At what age am I supposed to tell him the rest of these stories? The awful parts of our Old Testament heritage? The murder and incest and infidelity that littered chapters in the lives of these heroes and their violent Hebrew God?*

At the time, the right thing seemed to be to press ahead with the ark animals' two-by-two routine, and so that's what we did. That's what my mom did. Maybe yours did too. What else do you say to a three-year-old? God let the entire planet drown?

Regardless of how you read or interpret Scripture, constructs and framework are essential for early understanding of faith. Richard Rohr

This is what a life of faith looks like to me sometimes. *Longing for beauty.* Longing to build something that resembles *grace.* Recognizing my own limitations, but feeling the gaze of a *loving Creator* over my shoulder.

> We watch closely. We pray fervently for guidance.
> We make room for the difficult conversations,
> contradictions, and even doubt.

would call them *containers*—necessary for holding the beginnings of our knowledge of who God is. The authentic God we are meant to encounter must eventually break and spill out of those containers, creating more space to experience and understand His nature than we were able to with our smaller, simpler containers.

The early containers are the easy part of our job, right? Simple songs. Bedtime prayers. Love the Lord your God with all your heart, with all your soul, and with all your mind. Love your neighbor as yourself. Tell the truth. Be kind. Obey your parents. Learn about David's slingshot and the Red Sea parting and wonder if you'll be a shepherd or a wise man in this year's Christmas play.

A lot of adult Christian children will tell you that these are their favorite memories of their mothers' sweet spiritual instruction—perhaps their only. Sometimes (because growth is hard and gets harder) we may feel a strong temptation to keep the containers small—forever. For them. For us.

And if, like me, you grew up in a sheltered environment, where all school, family, church, and friendship interaction stayed in a pretty small faith container, it makes for a giant mess when that thing bursts. Confusion flows, and disillusion may follow.

How do we recognize when our children are spilling over the edges of their current spiritual understanding and ready for something roomier to contain it and to add to it as well? Add to it with deeper knowledge, harder questions, confusion or mystery, or even just silence.

We watch closely.

We pray fervently for guidance.

We don't allow our own containers to stay small. We make room for the difficult conversations, contradictions, and even doubt.

We remind our kids, when they venture out into unfamiliar or confusing or scary spiritual territory, that the contents of their new containers used to belong to the old.

When the Israelites were preparing to cross the River Jordan, high

Collect the stones. Hold sacred the stories of your journey with God, and stack them in front of your children as a reminder of what He has brought or is bringing you through.

and swollen, we read that when the feet of the priests stepped into the river, God dried up the water instantly. Carrying their sacred ark of the covenant, the entire nation crossed over a dry riverbed until they were safe on the other side.

When they had all crossed, Joshua instructed one man from each of the twelve tribes to collect a stone from the river to mark the place where God directed their safe passage. Joshua said to his people, "When your children ask in time to come, 'What do those stones mean to you?' then you shall tell them that the waters of the Jordan were cut off before the ark of the covenant of the LORD" (Joshua 4:6–7 ESV).

A pile of rocks—a reminder to tell the children and their children's children and generations to come of the goodness of God in that place.

This is one of our greatest callings.

Collect the stones. Hold sacred the stories of your journey with God, and stack them in front of your children as a reminder of what He has brought or is bringing you through. So when they ask, "What do these stones mean to you?" you will have an answer about the faithfulness of a vast and mysterious but deeply known God and a pile of broken containers to bear witness to what you have held—and what has held you. The containers may be smashed, but they were never empty. Tell them why.

Ask your kids to collect their own rocks too. Stack them up and allow them to fall. Dry tears at any age or stage, and remind them that every stone, every disappointment, every failure or foe or freedom testifies to something beautiful God is building in them. Slow and steady. Crossing the Jordan one step at a time.

These stacks of stones will never be pretty. They may never resemble a swan. But over time they may come to resemble an altar—an altar where you place every dream and desire you've ever had for your babies. Where you lay down all your own disappointments and delusions about what motherhood was supposed to be. All the joy and all the anguish laid out on that altar and given back to the God who was the very first to know that you would be someone's mom.

What do you these stones mean to you?

Everything.

acknowledgments

I continue to be so humbled by the number of people who have commented on the "Slow Down" video. I have cried many tears reading through the stories of beauty and heartache that are all part of this journey we call motherhood. Thank you to the thousands of strangers for sharing yourselves with me. Thank you to Brad O'Donnell at Capitol for gently insisting I record this song at all and to Chris Stevens for helping me shape it.

I'm incredibly grateful to work with this world-class team at Thomas Nelson. Their patience with me has been Herculean. Dawn Hollomon, you are an editor extraordinaire and such a joy to work with. MacKenzie Howard, you and your marvelous team were so helpful in shaping this so beautifully from the beginning.

As always, I am so indebted to my manager, Joel West at Method Management. You are a Godsend in every way. Thank you for not strangling me.

Gobs of gratitude for my friends and peers who contributed nuggets of wisdom from their own children's lives and hard-won mama wisdom: Natalie Grant, Patsy Clairmont, Amy Grant, Jessica Turner, Ellie Holcomb, Sara Groves, Shauna Niequist, and Jen Hatmaker. You are warriors who are constantly teaching me with your words, music, and lives.

Thank you, Shauna, for writing the beautiful forword. You are one of the moms I most deeply admire.

And an extra-long hug for my own mom, Penelope. May my children someday say about me even half the beautiful things I say about you. You are extraordinary. Love you a bushel and a peck.

Nichole Nordeman

EVERY MILE MATTERED

NEW STUDIO ALBUM FEATURING

"You're Here" & "Dear Me"

PLUS THE BONUS TRACK

"Slow Down"